THE U.S. NAVAL INSTITUTE ON

THE U.S. COAST GUARD

U.S. NAVAL INSTITUTE
WHEEL BOOKS

In the U.S. Navy, "Wheel Books" were once found in the uniform pockets of every junior and many senior petty officers. Each small notebook was unique to the Sailor carrying it, but all had in common a collection of data and wisdom that the individual deemed useful in the effective execution of his or her duties. Often used as a substitute for experience among neophytes and as a portable library of reference information for more experienced personnel, those weathered pages contained everything from the time of the next tide, to leadership hints from a respected chief petty officer, to the color coding of the phone-and-distance line used in underway replenishments.

In that same tradition, U.S. Naval Institute Wheel Books provide supplemental information, pragmatic advice, and cogent analysis on topics important to all naval professionals. Drawn from the U.S. Naval Institute's vast archives, the series combines articles from the Institute's flagship publication *Proceedings*, as well as selections from the oral history collection and from Naval Institute Press books, to create unique guides on a wide array of fundamental professional subjects.

THE U.S. NAVAL INSTITUTE ON

THE U.S. COAST GUARD

EDITED BY JIM DOLBOW

NAVAL INSTITUTE PRESS
Annapolis, Maryland

Naval Institute Press
291 Wood Road
Annapolis, MD 21402

Library of Congress Cataloging-in-Publication Data
Names: Dolbow, Jim, editor of compilation. | United States Naval Institute, issuing body.
Title: The U.S. Naval Institute on the U.S. Coast Guard / edited by Jim Dolbow.
Other titles: United States Naval Institute on the United States Coast Guard | US Naval Institute on the United States Coast Guard
Description: Annapolis, Maryland : Naval Institute Press, [2017] | Series: U.S. Naval Institute wheel books | Includes bibliographical references and index.
Identifiers: LCCN 2017022795 (print) | LCCN 2017026322 (ebook) | ISBN 9781591142300 (ePDF) | ISBN 9781591142300 (epub) | ISBN 9781591142300 (mobi) | ISBN 9781591142294 (pbk. : alk. paper) | ISBN 9781591142300 (ebook)
Subjects: LCSH: United States. Coast Guard. | United States. Coast Guard—History.
Classification: LCC VG53 (ebook) | LCC VG53 .U582 2017 (print) | DDC 363.28/60973—dc23
LC record available at https://lccn.loc.gov/2017022795

♾ Print editions meet the requirements of ANSI/NISO z39.48-1992 (Permanence of Paper). Printed in the United States of America.

25 24 23 22 21 20 19 18 17 9 8 7 6 5 4 3 2 1
First printing

CONTENTS

EDITOR'S NOTE

Because this book is an anthology, containing documents from different time periods, the selections included here are subject to varying styles and conventions. Other variables are introduced by the evolving nature of the Naval Institute's publication practices. For those reasons, certain editorial decisions were required in order to avoid introducing confusion or inconsistencies and to expedite the process of assembling these sometimes disparate pieces.

Gender

Many of the included selections were written when the armed forces were primarily a male domain and so adhere to purely masculine references. I have chosen to leave the original language intact in these documents for the sake of authenticity and to avoid the complications that can arise when trying to make anachronistic adjustments. So readers are asked to "translate" (converting the ubiquitous "he" to "he or she" and "his" to "her or his" as required) and, while doing so, to celebrate the progress that we have made in these matters in more recent times.

Author "Biographies"

Another problem arises when considering biographical information of the various authors whose works make up this special collection. Some of the selections included in this anthology were originally accompanied by biographical information about their authors. Others were not. Those "biographies" that do exist vary a great deal in terms of length and depth, some amounting to a single sentence pertaining to the author's current duty station, others consisting of several paragraphs that cover the author's career. Varying degrees of research—some quite time consuming and some yielding no results—are required to find biographical information from other sources. Because of these uneven variables, and because as a general rule we are more interested in what these authors have to say than who they are or were, I have chosen to even the playing field by foregoing accompanying "biographies." Relevant biographical information has been included in some of the accompanying commentaries, however.

Ranks

I have retained the ranks of the authors *at the time of the selection's original publication.* Some of the authors wrote early in their careers, and the sagacity of their earlier contributions says much about the individuals, about the significance of the Naval Institute's forum, and about the importance of writing to the naval services—something that is sometimes underappreciated.

Deletions

Most of the selections included here are intact, appearing as they originally did in their entirety, but in a few cases, some portions have been excerpted because the entire selection is too long to be included here. When these deletions have occurred, the following has been inserted: . . .

Other Anomalies

Readers may detect some inconsistencies in editorial style, reflecting staff changes at the Naval Institute, evolving practices in publishing itself, and various other factors not always identifiable. Some of the selections will include citation support, others will not. Authors sometimes coined their own words and occasionally violated traditional style conventions. *Bottom line:* with the exception of the removal of some extraneous materials (such as section numbers from book excerpts) and the conversion to a consistent font and overall design, these articles and excerpts appear as they originally did when first published.

INTRODUCTION

This Wheel Book is an anthology about the United States Coast Guard. The content for this book has been mined from the vast archives of *Proceedings* and the Naval Institute Press. Compiling it into this Wheel Book has been a labor of love for me.

The U.S. Naval Institute's intellectual content is equal to all of the gold at Fort Knox, in my humble opinion. Thumbing through the pages of back issues of *Proceedings* to find just the right article was a much tougher mission than I envisioned when I took on this assignment at the request of two great Americans, Rick Russell and Tom Cutler, director of the Naval Institute Press and the Gordon England Chair of Professional Naval Literature, respectively.

It was very difficult to choose from so many great titles published by the Naval Institute Press or the countless superb articles that have appeared in the pages of *Proceedings* over the years. When I found the right article or book excerpt to include in this anthology, it was like winning the lottery. This anthology is not exhaustive of all the U.S. Naval Institute's intellectual content on the U.S. Coast Guard. Difficult decisions had to be made on what article or book excerpt made it into this Coast Guard Wheel Book.

A note about the composition and organization of the chapters that comprise this Wheel Book: I viewed every *Proceedings* article as a work of art instead of a "breathing" document. Therefore, I didn't edit any of the *Proceedings* articles or delete their footnotes because I didn't want to take away from their author's original intent.

I have organized this Wheel Book into two parts. The first part will provide you, the reader, with background information on the roles, organization, and history of the U.S. Coast Guard. The second part contains articles about the many important missions of the U.S. Coast Guard.

It is my expectation that this Wheel Book will make a contribution to your knowledge about the United States Coast Guard.

PART I

U.S. Coast Guard Background

1 "HISTORY"

(Selection from chapter 1 of *The Coast Guardsman's Manual, 11th Edition*)

Jim Dolbow

No book about the United States Coast Guard (USCG) would be complete without a chapter on its proud history and heritage since August 4, 1790. One of the best short histories of the USCG can be found in chapter 1 of *The Coast Guardsman's Manual, 11th Edition*. A complimentary copy of the "CGM" is given to every recruit at Coast Guard boot camp in Cape May, New Jersey. You now can read this chapter without having to square your meals or do dozens of push-ups.

"HISTORY"

(Selection from chapter 1 of *The Coast Guardsman's Manual, 11th Edition*) by Jim Dolbow (Naval Institute Press, 2017): 3–23.

Introduction

The U.S. Coast Guard is one of this nation's five armed services and seven uniformed services. It is also the only branch of the U.S. military within the Department of Homeland Security. The legal basis for the Coast Guard is Title 14 of the United States Code, which states: "The Coast Guard as established January 28, 1915, shall be a military service and a branch of the armed forces of the United States at all times."

As members of a military service, Coast Guardsmen are subject to the Uniform Code of Military Justice and receive the same pay and allowances as members of the same pay grades in their four sister services. In peacetime, the Coast Guard operates under the Department of Homeland Security and the commandant of the Coast Guard reports to the secretary of Homeland Security. In time of war or when directed by the president, the Coast Guard operates as a service within the Department of the Navy.

By being aware of the Coast Guard's proud history and heritage, you will be able to understand where the Coast Guard is going and how you can best fit in. Remember, the operations and missions of today will be the history of tomorrow. You have an important part to play in helping preserve and promote our history and heritage for future generations.

Coast Guard history can be viewed as a series of important but unrelated events that can be selectively presented because they establish precedents, reinforce traditions, provide a neat comparison with another military organization, or have some special local interest. The Coast Guard is rich in this kind of history, and it encourages pride in our service.

The history of the service is very complicated because it is the amalgamation of five federal agencies. These agencies—the Revenue Cutter Service, the Lighthouse Service, the Steamboat Inspection Service, the Bureau of Navigation, and the Life-Saving Service—were originally independent but had overlapping authorities and were shuffled around the government. They sometimes received new names, and they were all finally united under the umbrella of the Coast Guard. The multiple missions and responsibilities of the modern service are directly tied to this diverse heritage and the magnificent achievements of all of these agencies.

One of the first orders of business our nation's founders had to contend with was maritime trade. In those days, almost all trade beyond the borders of the United States was done by ships. The following timeline reflects the many organizational changes of the predecessor agencies and when they became part of what is now the United States Coast Guard as well as changes in the organizational structure of the Coast Guard itself:

7 August 1789 The service, eventually to be known as the U.S. Lighthouse Service, was established under the control of the Treasury Department.

4 August 1790 This date is important to the Coast Guard because it is celebrated as the Coast Guard's birthday. Congress authorized Secretary of the Treasury Alexander Hamilton to create a maritime service to enforce customs laws. It didn't have an official name. It was simply referred to as "the cutters" or "the system of cutters." Hamilton established this fleet to enforce tariff laws, so these cutters were armed but manned by civilian crews under the Treasury Department. Since the Continental Navy was disbanded in 1785, there was no navy initially under the Constitution, and the cutters were the only maritime force available to the new government. Between 1790 and 1798 Hamilton's cutters were the only armed vessels protecting the coast, trade, and maritime interests of the new republic.

7 July 1838 A service to "provide better security of the lives of passengers on board of vessels propelled in whole or in part by steam" was established under the control of the Justice Department. This service later became the Steamboat Inspection Service.

14 August 1848 Congress appropriated funds to pay for lifesaving equipment to be used by volunteer organizations.

30 August 1852 The Steamboat Act established the Steamboat Inspection Service under the control of the Treasury Department.

9 October 1852 The Lighthouse Board, which administered the nation's lighthouse system until 1 July 1910, was organized.

18 June 1878 The U.S. Life-Saving Service was established as a separate agency under the control of the Treasury Department.

18 June 1878 Congress enacted the Posse Comitatus Act. This act limited military involvement in civilian law enforcement, leaving the Revenue Cutter Service as the only service branch consistently charged with federal law enforcement on the high seas and U.S. waters.

5 July 1884 The Bureau of Navigation was established under the control of the Treasury Department.

14 February 1903 The Department of Commerce and Labor was created. The Bureau of Navigation and the Steamship Inspection Service were transferred to the new department.

28 January 1915 President Woodrow Wilson signed into law the Act to Create the Coast Guard, an act passed by Congress on 20 January 1915 and combining the Life-Saving Service and Revenue Cutter Service to form the U.S. Coast Guard.

6 April 1917 With the declaration of war against Germany, the Coast Guard was transferred by executive order to the control of the Navy Department.

28 August 1919 The Coast Guard reverted to the Treasury Department after President Wilson signed Executive Order 3160.

30 June 1932 The Steamboat Inspection Service and the Bureau of Navigation were combined to form the Bureau of Navigation and Steamboat Inspection. The new agency remained under Commerce Department control.

27 May 1936 Public Law 622 reorganized and changed the name of the Bureau of Navigation and Steamboat Inspection Service to the Bureau of Marine Inspection and Navigation. The bureau remained under Commerce Department control.

1 July 1939 The Lighthouse Service became part of the Coast Guard.

19 February 1941 The Coast Guard Reserve was established by the passage of the Coast Guard Reserve and Auxiliary Act on this date. This legislation also established the Coast Guard Auxiliary under its present name (the Coast Guard Auxiliary had originally been called the Coast Guard Reserve). The new Coast Guard Reserve was modeled after the Naval Reserve as a military component. It was composed of two broad classifications: regular reservists and temporary reservists.

1 November 1941 President Franklin Roosevelt's Executive Order 8929 transferred the Coast Guard to Navy Department control.

28 February 1942 Executive Order 9083 transferred the Bureau of Marine Inspection temporarily to the Coast Guard under Navy Department control.

23 November 1942 Congress enacted Public Law 77-773 establishing the Women's Reserve as a branch of the Coast Guard. Members of this branch became known as SPARs, an acronym drawn from the service's motto, "Semper Paratus, Always Ready."

1 January 1946 In compliance with Executive Order 9666, the Coast Guard was returned to Treasury Department control.

April 1946 The Coast Guard created the Eastern, Western, and Pacific Area commands to coordinate cases that required the assets of more than one district.

16 July 1946 Pursuant to Executive Order 9083 and Reorganization Plan No. 3, the Bureau of Marine Inspection was abolished and became a permanent part of the Coast Guard under Treasury Department control.

1 April 1967 The Coast Guard was transferred from the Treasury Department to the newly created Department of Transportation.

January 1973 The Coast Guard renamed the Eastern and Western Areas to the Atlantic and Pacific Areas, respectively.

28 December 2001 The Coast Guard became the newest member of the U.S. Intelligence Community (IC) with the signing into law of the Intelligence Authorization Act for Fiscal Year 2002, which mandated the inclusion of the Coast Guard's national intelligence element formally into the IC.

1 March 2003 The Coast Guard was formally transferred from the Department of Transportation to the newly created Department of Homeland Security (DHS).

2004 To create unity of command in America's ports, better align field command structures, and improve Coast Guard operational effectiveness, sector commands were created throughout the Coast Guard by integrating groups, marine safety offices (MSOs), vessel traffic services (VTSs), and, in some cases, air stations.

2013 The U.S. Coast Guard Cyber Command (CGCYBERCOM) was established to provide cyber capabilities that foster excellence in the execution of Coast Guard operations, support DHS cyber missions, and serve as the Service Component Command to U.S. Cyber Command.

While the Coast Guard has undergone many changes over the years, it never stopped the Coast Guard and its predecessor agencies from answering our nation's call to duty.

The Coast Guard at War

Coast Guardsmen and their forefathers have fought in every war since the ratification of the U.S. Constitution. The U.S. Coast Guard standard proudly exhibits forty-three battle streamers, each one designed to remind us of our proud history and heritage. Many of the men and women who served our country in these wars sacrificed their lives for us, who now enjoy the freedoms they so jealously guarded. This record of military operations can be traced back to the Quasi-War with France and brought forward to today's war against terrorism.

Quasi-War of 1798–1800

Aggressive military and naval activity by France resulted in the seizure of several merchant vessels by armed French vessels on the high seas. The naval response of the United States was to employ the revenue cutters in the defense of our merchant fleet. In these operations, the cutters responded effectively, as they would in future conflicts in support of the nation's naval missions. Especially outstanding were the *Pickering*, COMO Edward Preble's first command, and the *Eagle*. The *Eagle* fought a memorable engagement with the French privateer *La Vengeance* (*Revenge*) in 1799, recapturing the American vessels *Nancy* and *Mehitable*.

War of 1812

From 1801 until the war with England in 1812, the cutters were busy enforcing the Embargo and Non-Intercourse Acts. After the War of 1812 began, the cutter *Jefferson* captured the first enemy prize in June. The cutter *Vigilant* captured the *Dart*. The most famous action was fought by the cutter *Eagle*. When she was caught by two British ships, her captain ran the ship ashore on Long Island. The crew dragged guns to a cliff top and beat off the enemy. That night they refloated their ship and headed for New Haven, Connecticut, but she could make little speed and the enemy finally captured her.

The end of the war brought no peace for the cutters. For the next quarter century, they fought pirates, slavers, smugglers, and Indians. The *Alabama* and *Louisiana* broke up the notorious Lafitte gang of pirates in the Gulf of Mexico, and the *Dallas* and *Jackson* fought the Seminole Indians in Florida.

Seminole Wars

During the Seminole Wars (1835–42) eight revenue cutters supported Army and Navy operations. Duties performed by these vessels included attacks on war parties, breaking up rendezvous points, picking up survivors of Seminole raids, carrying dispatches, transporting troops, blocking rivers to the passage of Seminole forces, and dispatching landing parties and artillery for the defense of settlements. These duties were performed along the entire coast of Florida.

Mexican War

The two principal naval operations carried out during the Mexican War (1846–48) were amphibious landings and blockading the enemy's coasts. The U.S. Navy was critically short of the shallow-draft vessels needed for the landings. Five cutters were engaged in amphibious operations and performed important services during a number of landings, particularly those at Alvarado and Tabasco. Cutters also served on blockade duty.

Civil War

The sympathies of the cutter force were divided between the North and the South during the American Civil War (1861–65). In a famous dispatch to Treasury Department agents, Secretary of the Treasury John A. Dix ordered, "If any one attempts to haul down the American flag, shoot him on the spot." Transmitted on the evening of 15 January 1861, this order was to ensure federal control of the cutter *Robert McClelland*, then in the port of New Orleans. Despite this message, many cutter men, including those on the *Robert McClelland*, chose to join the Confederacy. It was at this time that the service received its first official name, the Revenue Cutter Service.

The principal wartime duties of Union cutters were patrolling for commerce raiders and providing fire support for troops ashore. Meanwhile, Confederate cutters were principally used as commerce raiders. Cutters were also involved in notable individual actions. The first naval shot of the Civil War was fired by the cutter *Harriet Lane* when it challenged the steamer *Nashville* with a shot across its bow. The steamer was attempting to enter Charleston harbor without displaying the U.S. flag. The *Harriet Lane* also took part in the capture of Hatteras Inlet. Following this action, the cutter was transferred to the Navy. The cutter *Miami* carried President Abraham Lincoln and his party to Fort Monroe in May 1862, preparatory to the Peninsular Campaign. *Reliance*'s commanding officer was killed as the cutter engaged Confederate forces on the Great Wicomico River in 1864. On 21 April 1865 cutters were ordered to search all outbound ships for the assassins of President Lincoln. During the Civil War, 219 Revenue Cutter Service officers served, and 1 officer was killed in action.

Spanish-American War

The Revenue Cutter Service also rendered conspicuous service during the Spanish-American War (1898). Eight cutters carrying forty-three guns were in ADM William Sampson's fleet and on the Havana blockade. The *McCulloch*, with a complement of ten officers and ninety-five men and carrying six guns, was at the Battle of Manila Bay and was later employed by ADM George Dewey as his dispatch boat.

In the action off Cardenas on 11 May 1898, the cutter *Hudson*, LT Frank H. Newcomb commanding, sustained the fight against Spanish gunboats and shore batteries side by side with the torpedo boat USS *Winslow*. When half of *Winslow*'s crew had been killed and its commander wounded, *Hudson* rescued the torpedo boat from certain destruction. In recognition of this act of heroism,

Congress authorized a gold medal for Lieutenant Newcomb, a silver medal for each of the officers, and a bronze medal for the enlisted members of the crew.

Also during the Spanish-American War, the Navy assigned the task of coast watching to the U.S. Life-Saving Service. As a result, approximately two-thirds of the Navy's coastal observation stations were Life-Saving stations. Although the Spanish fleet never approached the U.S. coast, this Coast Guard predecessor service dutifully maintained its vigilance throughout the war. During the Spanish-American War 660 Revenue Cutter Service personnel served, with one fatality due to enemy action.

World War I

The outbreak of World War I in Europe in the summer of 1914 saw cutters become responsible for enforcing U.S. neutrality laws. It also marked the first time the Coast Guard was transferred to the Navy Department in wartime. The Coast Guard augmented the Navy with 47 vessels of all types and 279 stations scattered along the entire United States coastline. It was in this same period that Coast Guard aviation was born. LT E. F. Stone, USCG, one of several early Coast Guard flyers, was copilot on the Navy NC-4 flying boat, the first aircraft to cross the Atlantic.

During World War I, the Coast Guard continued to enforce rules and regulations that governed the anchorage and movements of vessels in American harbors. The Espionage Act, passed in June 1917, gave the Coast Guard further power to protect merchant shipping from sabotage. This act included the responsibility to safeguard waterfront property, supervise vessel movements, and establish anchorages and restricted areas, and the right to control and remove people on board ships.

A large number of Coast Guard officers held important commands during World War I. Twenty-four commanded naval warships in the war zone, five commanded warships attached to the American Patrol detachment in the Caribbean Sea, twenty-three commanded warships attached to naval districts, and five Coast Guard officers commanded large training camps. Six were assigned to aviation duty; two of those commanded important air stations including one in France. Shortly after the armistice in 1918, four Coast Guard officers were assigned to command large naval transports engaged to bring the troops home from France. Officers not assigned to command served in practically every phase of naval activity, on transports, cruisers, cutters, patrol vessels, in naval districts, as inspectors, and at training camps.

During World War I, 8,835 men served in the Coast Guard. Of those, 192 would pay the ultimate price due to combat, accident, or illness, to include the 115 crew members and 16 passengers on board USCGC *Tampa*, which was sunk on September 26, 1918—the largest loss of life on any U.S. combat vessel during World War I.

World War II

In World War II Coast Guardsmen operated escort destroyers, frigates, corvettes, patrol boats, and sub chasers, while planes patrolled the coasts and assisted in antisubmarine warfare. Beach patrols and port security units ensured coastal safety.

Immediately after the Japanese attack on Pearl Harbor on 7 December 1941, cutters were ordered to escort duty. This included going into action against Adolf Hitler's vaunted submarine fleet, nicknamed "hearses" by the Coast Guardsmen who fought them to the death on the open seas. During the war the U.S. Navy credited Coast Guard forces with sinking or assisting in the sinking of thirteen of Hitler's U-boats, although the number was probably only eleven. In the Pacific the Navy credited Coast Guard warships with sinking one Japanese submarine, but they probably sank two. Coast Guardsmen also captured two Nazi surface vessels, and they can take pride in knowing that they were the only United States service to do so during World War II. Additionally, two U-boats surrendered to Coast Guard–manned warships at the end of hostilities, including one, *U-234*, that was bound for Japan transporting a cargo of uranium and the latest German rocket and jet technology.

In the Pacific war, amphibious operations employed thousands of Coast Guardsmen, where their small-boat experience proved invaluable. Coast Guardsmen served on combat ships and in the support forces, where they manned naval transports, attack transports, supply vessels, and shore units.

During World War II 241,093 men and women served in the Coast Guard. Of these, 1,917 died, a third losing their life in action; 4 members of the Coast Guard were held as prisoners of war. The personnel strength of the Coast Guard peaked in 1944. Headquarters reported that as of 30 June 1944, there were 9,874 commissioned officers, 3,291 warrant officers, and 164,560 enlisted personnel serving in the regular and reserve (not including the Temporary Reserve or Auxiliary). Almost 2,000 Coast Guardsmen were decorated. Douglas Munro, a signalman, was posthumously awarded the only Medal of Honor earned by a member of the Coast Guard. He heads a long list of Coast Guard personnel who were cited for courage during World War II. The Coast Guard returned to the Treasury Department on 1 January 1946.

Korean War

In 1946 a Coast Guard team was sent to Seoul, Korea, to organize, supervise, and train a Korean coast guard. This Korean group became the National Maritime Police. A shipyard was set up, a supply and communications system was arranged, training facilities were established, and nineteen ships were transferred to Korea from the Japanese and U.S. navies.

With the outbreak of the Korean War (1950–53), marked by the invasion by North Korean Communist forces southward across the thirty-eighth parallel into the Republic of South Korea on 25 June 1950, the U.S. Coast Guard performed a variety of tasks. The Coast Guard established air detachments throughout the Pacific. These detachments, located at Sangley Point in the Philippines and in Guam, Wake, Midway, Adak, and Barbers Point in the Hawaiian Islands, conducted search and rescue to safeguard the tens of thousands of troops that were being airlifted across the Pacific.

The Coast Guard manned a number of Navy destroyer escorts, performing a variety of missions in the Western Pacific. A chain of mobile LORAN (long-range navigation) stations was established in the Far East to support the air and sea navigational needs of UN forces. One of those Coast Guard stations was situated at Pusan, South Korea. The Coast Guard also provided communications and meteorological services, plus ensured port security and proper ammunition handling.

The Coast Guard remained under the Department of the Treasury throughout the Korean War. Eight thousand five hundred Coast Guardsmen were eligible for the Korean Service Medal. There were no Coast Guard casualties in the Korean War.

Vietnam War

At the outset of the Vietnam War the Navy lacked shallow-water craft needed for inshore operations. To help fill this need, the Coast Guard sent twenty-six eighty-two-foot cutters to Vietnam. The cutters spent some 70 percent of their time under way. They inspected junks for contraband, intercepted and destroyed North Vietnamese and Viet Cong craft, and provided fire support for friendly forces.

While the eighty-two-foot cutters helped patrol inshore, larger cutters were needed to form a deep-water barrier against infiltration. For this task, the Coast Guard deployed high-endurance cutters. Thirty high-endurance cutters served on this duty between 1967 and 1971.

The U.S. Army had the difficult task of setting up harbor security and getting cargo safely unloaded and moved into the country. Since almost all munitions entered South Vietnam by ship, the Army asked for the assistance of the Coast Guard. The men of the Coast Guard Port Security and Waterways Detail traveled throughout Vietnam inspecting ports and harbors for security against enemy attack and for the safe storage of hazardous materials. Coast Guard explosives loading detachments were established at major ports to supervise the offloading of ships.

The Coast Guard also set up and operated a LORAN-C system in Southeast Asia in order to assist the U.S. Air Force warplanes with precision navigation. It was a difficult task finding transmitting sites, bringing in equipment, and building the system. LORAN stations were established in Lampang, Sattahip, and Udorn, Thailand, and in Con Son, Vietnam. A fifth station was later added in Tan My, Vietnam.

The rapid development of deep-water ports in Vietnam brought an expanded need for navigational aids to prevent vessel accidents. South Vietnam's small aids-to-navigation force, with its one buoy tender, could not meet the demand. Coast Guard buoy tenders in the Pacific made periodic trips to Vietnam installing and maintaining buoys. A Coast Guard aids-to-navigation detail was set up in Saigon to coordinate workloads for these visits as well as to keep buoys and range markers lighted.

At the height of the war more than three hundred merchant ships were engaged in the sealift of matériel to Vietnam. The Coast Guard Merchant Marine Detail resolved merchant seaman problems and ensured that these ships moved in and out with as little delay as possible.

Coast Guard pilots flew combat search and rescue with the Air Force in Southeast Asia, under an interservice exchange program that was initiated in 1967. Most of the time, the pilots were assigned to the 37th Aerospace Rescue and Recovery Squadron at Danang. They flew Sikorsky HH-3F "Jolly Green Giants" in some of the most dangerous operations undertaken during the war. LT Jack Rittichier (Coast Guard Aviator #997) became the first Coast Guardsman to die from enemy action in Vietnam when his helicopter was shot down on 9 June 1968 during an attempt to pull a downed Marine Corps pilot from enemy-held territory.

Some eight thousand Coast Guardsmen served in Vietnam. Seven lost their lives and sixty were wounded.

Operations Desert Shield and Desert Storm

On 2 August 1990 Iraq invaded the country of Kuwait. A coalition of countries from around the world, led by the United States, quickly responded to this invasion. The Coast Guard's unique operational capabilities and maritime expertise were tapped quickly and often by the Departments of Defense, State, and Transportation, and by governments of the Allied Coalition.

On 22 August 1990 President George H. W. Bush authorized the call-up of members of the selected reserve to active duty in support of Operation Desert Shield. Three port security units (PSUs) consisting of a total of 550 Coast Guard reservists were deployed to Saudi Arabia in support of Operation Desert Shield to provide for waterside security. (This was the first involuntary overseas mobilization of Coast Guard Reserve PSUs in the Coast Guard Reserve's fifty-year history.) Law enforcement detachments were dispatched to augment and most often lead the naval boarding teams enforcing the UN economic embargo. These teams conducted hundreds of boardings and uncovered tons of illicit cargo. Moreover, during Operation Desert Shield, the initial Coast Guard efforts included breaking out sixty-eight ships of the Ready Reserve and locating merchant seamen to safely sail the vessels. The loading of hazardous materials and ammunition was supervised in U.S. ports.

Coast Guard personnel also augmented the staff of the Commander, Middle East Forces to coordinate interdiction and search-and-rescue (SAR) efforts of the myriad naval forces deployed in the Persian Gulf and Red Sea. Coast Guard oil-spill experts quickly responded to a request from the Saudi Arabian government to assist them in dealing with the massive oil spill. These experts and Aireye-equipped aircraft provided invaluable technical advice and assistance in combating this act of environmental terrorism.

With the commencement of offensive action against the forces of Iraq under the auspices of Operation Desert Storm on 17 January 1991, Coast Guard Marine Safety Offices increased both the level and tempo of port safety and security activities in the port to protect critical commercial and military waterfront facilities from the threat of terrorism. The Coast Guard increased both shoreside and waterside security patrols in ports using regular and reserve augmentation forces and established and enforced waterside security zones around key facilities.

Operations Support Democracy and Uphold Democracy

From November 1993 to August 1995 (Operation Support Democracy) and October 1994 to March 1995 (Operation Uphold Democracy), Coast Guard cutters and port security units supported UN-led operations to restore democratic institutions in Haiti. Two port security units, a harbor defense unit, five law enforcement detachments, and thirteen cutters carried out operations that included conducting maritime surveillance and interdiction, providing search-and-rescue coverage for in-transit U.S. aircraft, and establishing and restoring aids to navigation.

Operation Allied Force

Operation Allied Force was the seventy-eight-day NATO air campaign from 24 March 1999 to 10 June 1999 against Serbian military targets in the former Federal Republic of Yugoslavia. USCGC *Bear* (WMEC-901) deployed to the Adriatic Sea in support of Operation Allied Force as part of USS *Theodore Roosevelt* (CVN-71) battle group. *Bear* provided surface surveillance and SAR response for the Sea Combat Commander, and force protection for the Amphibious Ready Group that operated near Albania. *Bear* provided combat escort for U.S. Army vessels transporting military cargo between Italy and Albania. This escort operation took *Bear* up to the Albanian coastline, well within enemy surface-to-surface missile range.

9/11

On 11 September 2001 terrorists from the al-Qaeda network hijacked four commercial aircraft, crashing two into the World Trade Center in New York and one into the Pentagon in Washington, D.C. (The fourth aircraft crashed around Shanksville, Pennsylvania, when passengers on board attempted to regain control of the aircraft from the terrorists.) USCG units from New York City were among the first military units to respond in order to provide security and render assistance to those in need.

In response to the terrorist threat and to protect our nation's coastline, ports, and waterways, six U.S. Navy *Cyclone*-class patrol coastal warships were assigned to Operation Noble Eagle on 5 November 2001. This was the first time that U.S. Navy ships were employed jointly under Coast Guard command.

In response to 9/11, President George W. Bush proposed the establishment of the Department of Homeland Security. The Coast Guard was slated to be transferred from the Department of Transportation to the new department.

On 25 November 2002 President Bush signed HR 5005, creating the Department of Homeland Security. Soon after, Tom Ridge, former governor of Pennsylvania, was confirmed as the department's first secretary. On 25 February 2003 Transportation Secretary Norman Mineta transferred leadership of the U.S. Coast Guard to Secretary Ridge, formally recognizing the change in civilian leadership over the Coast Guard and ending the Coast Guard's almost thirty-six-year term as a member of the Department of Transportation. As a result of the attacks, homeland security moved to the forefront of the service's primary missions.

Operation Iraqi Freedom

Coast Guard forces deployed to Southwest Asia in support of the U.S.-led coalition engaged in Operation Iraqi Freedom early in 2003. Coast Guard vessels and land-based personnel brought many vital capabilities to the theater of operations, including inshore patrol and port security. At the height of operations there were 1,250 Coast Guard personnel deployed, including about 500 reservists. The forces also included two large cutters, a buoy tender, eight patrol boats, four port security units, law enforcement detachments, and support staff to the U.S. Central Command and U.S. European Command.

On 25 April 2004 DC3 Nathan Bruckenthal, USCG, from Smithtown, New York, and two U.S. Navy sailors were killed in the line of duty while conducting maritime intercept operations in the North Arabian Gulf. Bruckenthal and six other coalition sailors had attempted to board a small boat near an Iraqi oil facility. As they boarded the boat, it exploded. Petty Officer Bruckenthal later died from injuries sustained in the explosion; he was the first Coast Guardsman killed in action since the Vietnam War. Bruckenthal had been assigned to Tactical Law Enforcement South in Miami, Florida, and had deployed with Coast Guard Patrol Forces Southwest Asia on board USS *Firebolt* (PC-10).

Disasters and Contingency Operations

Closer to home, the Coast Guard provides our nation with tremendous value in service to the public during times of natural and man-made disasters and other contingencies. A sampling of key domestic events and missions for the Coast Guard includes the following:

Sinking of the *Titanic*, 1912

Following the sinking of the *Titanic*, Congress authorized the International Ice Patrol.

Camarioca Boatlift, 1965

The Camarioca Boatlift was the first large-scale exodus of Cuban immigrants attempting to enter the United States. Thereafter, migrant interdiction became a policy concern.

Argo Merchant Oil Spill, 1976

The *Argo Merchant*, a Liberian tanker, grounded off Nantucket in December, carrying 7.3 million gallons of fuel oil. Coast Guard cutters *Sherman*, *Vigilant*, *Spar*, and *Bittersweet* were on the scene and prepared to use the air-deployable antipollution transfer system on the vessel. However, deteriorating weather, thirty-knot winds, and heavy seas prevented removal of its cargo before the hull began to buckle. The bow was wrenched from the hull and opened the cargo to the sea. This was the largest oil spill up until then in American waters. Northwesterly winds dispersed the oil out to sea. The *Argo Merchant* accident and fourteen more tanker accidents in or near American waters over the next ten weeks caused great concern about tanker safety.

Mariel Boatlift, 1980

Boats with Cuban migrants on board began departing Mariel, Cuba, in April 1980. The first two boats arrived in Miami on the same day, marking the largest Cuban migration to the United States. Cuban leader Fidel Castro then declared the port of Mariel "open," increasing the number of boats involved in the exodus and giving the exodus its name. By the time the boatlift came to an end in October 1980, more than 125,000 Cubans had made the journey to the United States. It was the largest search-and-rescue operation conducted by the Coast Guard since World War II and gave the service an indication of the increasing role the service would play regarding migrant interdiction in upcoming years.

Exxon Valdez Oil Spill, 1989

The *Exxon Valdez* oil spill led to the creation of the Oil Pollution Act of 1990 (OPA-90). In this act Congress addressed tanker construction, personnel licensing, and the emergency rapid-response capability. The act called for mandatory double hulls on new tankers and the gradual phasing out of noncomplying vessels. The licensing requirements for ship's officers were strengthened in the area of drug and alcohol testing. The rapid-response capability was expanded nationwide, and new emphasis was placed on oil pollution research. The act required the Coast Guard to create response groups (known as strike teams) capable of responding to spills and other disasters.

Hurricanes Katrina and Rita, 2005

Hurricane Katrina struck the Gulf of Mexico states on 29 August 2005, devastating a 90,000-square-mile area from Grand Isle, Louisiana, to Mobile, Alabama. It was one of the worst natural disasters in American history, with more than 1,200 deaths and $80 billion in property damage. The enormous storm surge and subsequent multiple levee breaches flooded more than 60 percent of New Orleans. Tens of thousands of men, women, and children were left stranded on rooftops and in city buildings with no food, water, or electricity.

The massive response that followed was the largest search-and-rescue operation in U.S. history. More than 5,000 Coast Guardsmen from around the country responded to more than 33,000 people. They also responded to thousands of oil spills totaling more than 9 million gallons, repaired navigational aids, and restored waterways in and around some of the country's most vital ports.

The Coast Guard has proven agility and significant experience in leading integrated joint-agency operations. Due largely to this, the Coast Guard's chief of staff was chosen to be the principal federal official in the early days of the disaster to coordinate the massive federal, state, and local responses to Hurricane Katrina and, subsequently, Hurricane Rita, which hit nearly the same area just one month later.

Hurricanes Katrina and Rita tested the Coast Guard's organizational character. These events once again illustrated our service's unique national value: Complementary missions and skills, core-value competencies, and deeply ingrained principles of operation enabled the Coast Guard to rise to the moment.

Haiti Earthquake, 2010

On 12 January 2010 a devastating 7.0 earthquake struck Haiti. The Coast Guard cutter *Forward* was diverted from a law enforcement patrol in the Caribbean and arrived in Port-au-Prince, Haiti, within seventeen hours of the disaster.

The cutter *Forward* provided the world with firsthand images and reports of the devastation that had struck the impoverished nation. The first helicopters on scene were from Coast Guard units deployed to the Turks and Caicos Islands for counternarcotics operations. More than eight hundred Coast Guard personnel, cutters, and aircraft were involved in response and relief efforts, including operations to evacuate injured personnel and U.S. citizens, and in delivery of aid. Coast Guard cutters and personnel also completed port assessments and developed plans to reconstitute port operations, allowing for safe transit of humanitarian supplies from relief ships to coastal logistics staging points.

Deepwater Horizon Oil Spill, 2010

On 20 April 2010 the Coast Guard responded to a distress call following an explosion on the Deepwater Horizon oil rig in the Gulf of Mexico. During the initial search-and-rescue response more than one hundred people were rescued. As the scope and focus of the incident expanded and shifted to the ensuing oil spill, the Coast Guard led the monumental federal response to the first ever Spill of National Significance and one of the worst environmental disasters in U.S. history. The scope of the unprecedented response involved more than seven thousand Coast Guard personnel, forty-six cutters and boats, and twenty-two aircraft. Throughout the incident, the Coast Guard led a whole of government and industry response to secure the wellhead, contain and clean up the spill, and protect the Gulf Coast ecosystem.

2 "COAST GUARD"

(Selection from chapter 31 of *The Naval Institute Guide to the Ships and Aircraft of the U.S. Fleet, 19th Edition*)

Norman Polmar

This excerpt from the Coast Guard chapter in Norman Polmar's *Ships and Aircraft of the U.S. Fleet, 19th Edition* is a good primer on the people, organization, and platforms (cutters, aircraft, and small boats) in today's U.S. Coast Guard.

"COAST GUARD"

(Selection from chapter 31 of *The Naval Institute Guide to the Ships and Aircraft of the U.S. Fleet, 19th Edition*) by Norman Polmar, (Naval Institute Press, 2013): 575–611.

The Coast Guard is a military, multi-mission service within the Department of Homeland Security. It is one of the five U.S. military services and the only one outside of the Department of Defense. Federal statute states that in the national security role the Coast Guard "shall maintain a state of readiness to function as a specialized service in the Navy in time of war, including the fulfillment of Maritime Defense Zone command responsibilities."

At the direction of the President, the Coast Guard can become a part of the Navy, as during World Wars I and II. Alternatively, it can operate in a war zone while remaining an independent service, as during the Korean and Vietnam Wars, the 1991 conflict in the Persian Gulf, and the 2003 invasion of Iraq. . . .

The Coast Guard owns or leases bases and facilities at more than 2,800 geographic locations in the United States and its territories. . . .

Organization

Coast Guard Headquarters, located in Washington, D.C., provides the overall supervision and support for the operating districts. The senior uniformed officer of the Coast Guard is the Commandant. . . .

The major U.S. Coast Guard operating commands are the Atlantic Area (headquarters in Portsmouth, Virginia) and the Pacific Area (headquarters in Alameda, California) with nine subordinate district commands. The area commanders are vice admirals; the district commanders are rear admirals.

The district commanders control all shore, air, and sea activities within their respective areas of responsibility. In addition, since 1985–86, the commanders of the Coast Guard Atlantic and Pacific areas are commanders of the Maritime Defense Zone (MDZ) Atlantic and Pacific, respectively. The MDZ commanders report to their respective Navy fleet commanders.

The MDZ commanders are responsible for (1) planning, conducting, and coordinating wartime operations in and around U.S. harbors and coasts; (2) ensuring the maintenance of an integrated defense plan for the MDZ areas of responsibility; and (3) protecting coastal and nearby sea lines of communication. Within each MDZ are operating sectors, which are commanded by Coast Guard district or base commanders. . . .

Personnel

Uniformed Coast Guard personnel operate all cutters and boats as well as aircraft. Medical personnel are provided by Public Health service personnel on assignment to the Coast Guard. . . .

Coast Guard personnel have Navy-style ranks. . . .

Operations

Coast Guard forces operate worldwide, with particular emphasis in U.S. waters, with "black-hull" ships and craft maintaining inland and coastal aids to navigation. Offshore operations—with "white-hull" ships and cutters—extend well

Table 31-1. COAST GUARD DISTRICTS

DISTRICT	HEADQUARTERS	AREA
Atlantic Area		
1st District	Boston, Mass.	Northeast
5th District	Portsmouth, Va.	Middle Atlantic
7th District	Miami, Fla.	Southeast
8th District	New Orleans, La.	Central-Gulf Coast, Midwest
9th District	Cleveland, Ohio	Northern-Great Lakes
Pacific Area		
11th District	Alameda, Calif.	Southwest
13th District	Seattle, Wash.	Northwest
14th District	Honolulu, Hawaii	Hawaii
17th District	Juneau, Alaska	Alaska

into oceanic waters, with emphasis off the U.S. West Coast and Caribbean, to deter illegal migrants and drug smuggling. . . .

The end of the Cold War and the subsequent campaigns against terrorism have seen an expansion of Coast Guard responsibilities and areas of activity. Increasingly, Coast Guard assets are sought for overseas operations by U.S. government and military leaders. These activities include, but are not limited to, training Third World naval and coast guard forces; carrying out liaison and joint operations with foreign navies and coast guards in the areas of law-enforcement, pollution control, resource protection, and anti-terrorism; and providing direct support of U.S. military operations.

The Coast Guard is especially suited for working with Third World and developing countries, many of whose navies are more analogous to the Coast Guard in terms of men, ships, and missions than they are to the Navy. In many of those countries the naval/coast guard missions are similar, if not the same—the enforcement of resources and fisheries regulations, law enforcement, search and rescue, river and waterways management, port security, maritime safety, etc. Thus, the Coast Guard—a military service—can work directly with those countries on a non-military basis. . . .

Cutters and Boats

The Coast Guard operates a large number of ocean-going, coastal, and inland ships and small craft for a variety of purposes. A major procurement program for ocean-going cutters, patrol boats, and aircraft is ongoing, known as the Integrated Deepwater System (IDS) project. This is the largest procurement program in Coast Guard history. . . .

Most cutters are painted white, the larger icebreakers are painted red, and buoy tenders and harbor tugs are painted black (with white superstructures). The Coast Guard "racing stripes" insignia, a narrow blue and wide red stripe, angled at 64 degrees, with the Coast Guard shield super-imposed on the latter, is carried on the bow of all cutters and boats. The words "Coast Guard" are painted on the sides of all ships and boats. . . .

The Coast Guard uses the term *vessels* for all watercraft operated by the service. Within that classification, the term *cutter* is used for ships that have "an assigned personnel allowance and that [have] installed habitability features for the extended support of a permanently assigned crew." In practice, this includes 65-foot tugs and larger vessels. The term cutter comes from the early British revenue service ships, which were cutter-rigged sailing vessels, although the original U.S. revenue cutters were sailing schooners.

Craft less than 65 feet in length are considered *boats* and have hull numbers in which the first two digits indicate the vessel's length overall. However, the designation *patrol boat* (WPB) is used for craft up to 123 feet.

The Coast Guard classifies all of its ships and small craft by length (in this chapter shown in parentheses after the class name). The Coast Guard vessel classification system is derived from the Navy's classification system. . . . The Coast Guard adopted the Navy's ship classification system—which dated to 1920—in February 1942, with each cutter being assigned a two- or three-letter designation and sequential hull number. Previously only small, unnamed cutters and former U.S. Navy destroyers in Coast Guard service had hull numbers. (Construction numbers were often used to distinguish the larger cutters.)

To differentiate them from their Navy counterparts, all Coast Guard cutters were given the prefix letter *W* in February 1942. There is no definitive explanation for the *W* prefix. A bureaucratic argument is that *W* was used during the 1930s as the routing symbol on Treasury Department correspondence to designate the Coast Guard; another is that it indicated "weather patrol," one of the major tasks assigned to the Coast Guard. The theory was also put forth that the *W* indicated white-painted ships, although by February 1942 all Coast Guard vessels had been seconded to naval service and were painted gray.

In 1965 the Coast Guard adopted its own designation system for larger cutters and for specialized vessels, e.g., buoy tenders (WAGL). The larger cutters were designated on the basis of their range/sea-keeping qualities—high-endurance (WHEC) and medium-endurance (WMEC). Smaller cutters retained their Navy-type designation, e.g., WPC, WPB. . . .

Aviation

The Coast Guard air arm has 211 aircraft in service and in storage. They are based at 18 Coast Guard Air Stations (CGAS) in the continental United States, plus one in Puerto Rico, one in Hawaii, and two in Alaska. . . .

Icebreakers

Coast Guard icebreakers operate in the Arctic and Antarctic regions in support of U.S. national requirements for military and scientific activities. The Coast Guard currently has two large icebreakers in service—one of the Polar class and one of the *Healy* class.

There is growing interest in Congress in increasing the Coast Guard's icebreaking capabilities as the shift in the Arctic ice pack has increased military, political, and economic interests in the region. The Coast Guard estimates that it requires at least three "heavy" and three "medium" icebreakers to meet minimum mission requirements as the polar ice pack recedes. . . .

Training Cutters

. . . The sail-training "cutter" *Eagle* is based at the Coast Guard Academy in New London; she is employed to train Coast Guard cadets on summer practice cruises.

She is the former German naval training barque *Horst Wessel.* Taken by the United States as reparation after World War II, she was acquired in January 1946 at Bremerhaven and assigned to the Coast Guard. . . .

. . . The *Eagle* is steel-hulled. She carries up to 21,350 square feet of sail.

Buoy Tenders

These ships maintain aids to navigation in U.S. coastal waters as well as on inland waterways.

All tenders are "black-hull" ships. . . .

Small Craft

The Coast Guard operates approximately 2,000 boats and small craft in the law enforcement, patrol, search-and-rescue, oil cleanup, and navigation support roles.

3 "TEAM COAST GUARD"

(Selection from part 3 of *A Coast Guardsman's History of the U.S. Coast Guard*)

C. Douglas Kroll

The men and women of the U.S. Coast Guard serve in a variety of capacities that are outlined in Douglas Kroll's *A Coast Guardsman's History of the U.S. Coast Guard.* His chapter on Team Coast Guard was selected because it is very succinct about the Coast Guard's active-duty, reserve, auxiliary, and civilian employees. Without all four components working together as Team Coast Guard, the U.S. Coast Guard would no longer be the world's greatest coast guard.

"TEAM COAST GUARD"

(Selections from Part 3 of *A Coast Guardsman's History of the U.S. Coast Guard*) by C. Douglas Kroll (Naval Institute Press, 2010): 95, 107, 117–18, and 127.

Team Coast Guard

The term "Team Coast Guard" has been used for several decades to refer to the active duty service, the Reserve, the Auxiliary, and civilian employees working together to accomplish the many missions of the Coast Guard.

But it was not until August 1994 that Adm. Robert E. Kramek, commandant of the Coast Guard, formally defined the term in a general message that spoke primarily of the relationship between the active duty and Reserve services, marking dramatic changes for the latter. The message disestablished all Coast Guard Reserve units except Harbor Defense Command and Port Security Units and sought to eliminate Reserve-only workspaces where active duty ones were more efficient. It shifted administrative support of Reservists from Reserve-only administration offices to integrated personnel support units. The majority of Reservists were from then on to be assigned to active duty commands.

The commandant's desire was for Team Coast Guard to have one set of missions, one command structure, and one administrating structure, and to fully integrate Reserve forces. The goal was the functional integration of the service. However, Team Coast Guard has now come to refer to all the elements listed earlier. Working together, these different team members enable the Coast Guard to accomplish much more than it could if acting with only the active-duty service. The Coast Guard Reserve and the Auxiliary have come to be seen as force multipliers. The entire team has acted together in responding to major disasters or operations. What follows are a few examples of that teamwork. . . .

Coast Guard Auxiliary

The U.S. Coast Guard Auxiliary is the uniformed civilian component of the Coast Guard. An organization of vetted and trained volunteers, the Auxiliary provides a broad inventory of vital skills, assets, and experience for Coast Guard units across the nation. It is an essential component of Team Coast Guard and directly supports the service in all missions except military and direct law enforcement actions.

Established in 1939 to involve experienced recreational boaters in promoting boating safety, the Auxiliary is now also a valuable force multiplier for the active duty service, which is tasked with new homeland security missions and is chronically underfunded by Congress. Overall, the Auxiliary accounts for some 12 percent of the Coast Guard's total search and rescue caseload. Auxiliarists teach public courses in seamanship, navigation, and other specialties. They provide free courtesy vessel safety checks of recreational boats to make sure they meet federal and state requirements. Besides conducting safety patrols in their own vessels, the Auxiliary also has a small aviation arm that flies surveillance and search and rescue patrols over coastal areas.

Auxiliary members are legally civilians not subject to the Uniform Code of Military Justice. They perform tasks that in the Coast Guard are usually carried out by enlisted personnel, and although they have no rank, they wear officers' uniforms and insignia (with a capital "A" embossed on them) to denote the most important elected or appointed position they've held in the Auxiliary. . . .

Coast Guard Reserve

By the 1930s, the Coast Guard was the only armed service that did not have a reserve component. The Army and Navy had sizable organizations of veterans and other personnel who were paid modest salaries to stay in training and make themselves available in a national emergency. With World War II under way in Asia and Europe, Congress passed the Coast Guard Reserve Act of 1939. However, this new Reserve was to be a civilian, volunteer organization focused primarily on assisting the Coast Guard in its boating safety responsibilities. Membership was limited to those who owned boats.

By 1941 the Coast Guard was preparing for war, and Congress restructured the Reserve. Henceforth the service would have two reserve forces. The existing civilian organization was renamed the Coast Guard Auxiliary, and a new military Coast Guard Reserve was created on 19 February 1941. The service Guard expanded to more than 214,000 active duty personnel by the peak of World War II. More than 92 percent were Reservists, serving in all theaters of the war.

As the war progressed, the Joint Chiefs of Staff, following the examples of Great Britain and the Soviet Union, realized women would have to play a major role in the war effort. Congress created the Women's Reserve of the Coast Guard in November 1942, modeled on the Navy's Women's Reserve that had been formed a few months earlier. Two restrictions placed on Navy women were carried over to the Coast Guard: women were not to serve outside the continental United States; and no woman, officer or enlisted, was empowered to issue orders to any male Coast Guardsman.

Women in the Coast Guard reserve were known by the acronym SPARs, based on the service's motto "Semper Paratus, Always Ready." Most SPAR officers received their training at the academy in New London, and most enlisted SPARs were trained at Palm Beach, Florida.

By 1943, the restriction on giving orders to Coast Guardsmen was abolished, and by September 1944 Congress also abolished overseas-duty restriction. By the end of the war, about 200 SPARs had served in Alaska, and 200 more in Hawaii. Altogether, approximately 11,000 women served in the Coast Guard Women's Reserve. Shortly after the surrender of Japan in 1945, women's reserve branches of all the services were disbanded. USCGC *Spar* (WLB-403) was commissioned on 12 June 1944 in honor of women reservists (and decommissioned in 1997). The last SPAR was discharged in 1947, although the label was still being applied to female Coast Guardsmen in the 1960s. In 2001 the service commissioned another ship by the same name, *Spar* (WLB-206), honoring all those who had served.

Coast Guard Civilian Employees

Frequently overlooked when talking about Team Coast Guard is the large number of civilian employees who, on a regular basis, make invaluable contributions to meeting the service's missions. There are some 8,000 civilian members of the Coast Guard (2,000 of whom are paid with non-appropriated funds) in 100 locations, representing more than 280 occupations. They are an essential part of the team. Civilians often work behind the scenes, away from the spotlight. But their presence is felt on cutters, small boats, and aircraft. Without them the cutters would not sail, the aircraft would not fly, and the stations would fall into disrepair.

Civilians have also played an extraordinarily important and fascinating part of Coast Guard history. Lifesaving missions, inspection functions, and many aids-to-navigation duties all were carried out at some time by civilians. Many of the legendary figures discussed in this book were not military but civilian. Today some civilians serve in a boardroom setting, developing strategic plans or representing the Coast Guard at top-level conferences. Members of the Senior Executive Service not only influence and shape the Coast Guard's future, they also play a leading role in managing current policies and programs.

4 "U.S. COAST GUARD AUXILIARY AVIATION: EXPANDABLE FORCE CAPABILITY"

Ron Darcey

Coast Guard Auxiliarist Darcey lays out in great detail the important role played by the Coast Guard's Auxiliary aircraft. With a fleet of nearly 180 volunteer aircraft, the Coast Guard Auxiliary is indeed a force multiplier for a resource-strained U.S. Coast Guard. Besides delivering much-deserved recognition for the U.S. Coast Guard Auxiliary's fleet of aircraft, this article was selected because it outlines the full potential of volunteer aircraft in the Coast Guard Auxiliary.

"U.S. COAST GUARD AUXILIARY AVIATION: EXPANDABLE FORCE CAPABILITY"

By Ron Darcey, U.S. Naval Institute *Proceedings* (August 2010): 77–79.

The U.S. Coast Guard's joint-force capability consists entirely of uniformed civilian volunteers serving in nearly every operational mission except law enforcement and combat. Most recognize the Coast Guard Auxiliary as a surface or float organization, but fewer are aware of the aviation element that, while comparatively small, acts as a vital strategic multiplier.

With an average of 180 aircraft nationally, Auxiliary Aviation (AuxAir) expands operations, increases force capability, and reinforces operational flexibility. Today, particularly after the service's transfer from the Department of Transportation to the Department of Homeland Security (DHS), the Auxiliary is being tasked with increasing mission responsibilities beyond the organization's traditional operations of recreational boating safety, education, and training.

Over the years, Auxiliary Aviation has matured into a well-trained organization, recognized and deployed as an important strategic and tactically capable asset flying small, private aircraft. It combines excellent handling, performance, and economy for a multitude of Coast Guard and DHS missions.

Unfortunately, many still do not understand the benefits that Auxiliary Aviation has available. In fact, many Coast Guard personnel are unaware that AuxAir even exists.

Recreational Boating Safety, Education, Search and Rescue

The Auxiliary was formed to provide recreational boating safety, small-vessel checks, boating education, search and rescue, and nationwide administrative support and reinforcement activities at Coast Guard facilities. Its role in boating safety is highly relevant in supporting the service in its enormous mission of monitoring a national average of 17 million registered pleasure craft navigating our shorelines, lakes, and waterways.

Search and rescue has always been an Auxiliary specialty, a mission performed exceptionally well during and especially after active-duty colleagues have ended the operation. Auxiliarists often continue the search and just as often successfully locate victims for rescue. Of considerable value, Auxiliarists, because they live and work in their area of responsibility, are intimate with the geography and climate where they patrol. They require no specialized area familiarization.

Coast Guard Auxiliary Aviation

With aviation capability being a primary extension of Coast Guard operations, airplanes flown by Auxiliary aviators complement that capability. Auxiliary Air was created by legislative action in September 1944, as Jesse F. England became the first AuxAir aviator. He was soon followed by eight pilots and aircraft at Glenrock Airport, Norfolk, Virginia, forming Flotilla 2, Fifth Coast Guard District. Over the years, other private pilots and observers have joined the air program that today includes more than 500 Auxiliary aviators.

Private, general-aviation aircraft are ideally suited for a wide range of operations in the traditional role of search and rescue, but are particularly valuable today for many tasks not previously considered part of the AuxAir mission. At between 1,000 and 2,000 feet, Auxiliary flight crews watch over bays, ports, harbors, bridges, and causeways; they stand guard over illegal immigrant interdiction; and they monitor large-vessel traffic transiting littoral waters and steaming through deepwater inland shipping channels.

Each Coast Guard district air station is responsible for deployment of its AuxAir component. Daily missions differ from district to district, as do mission assignments, relative to operational requirements and priorities. Most important is the use of AuxAir on lower-priority missions, which conserves Coast Guard aviation assets and allows air-station concentration on hazardous or specialized missions and training.

Auxiliary aircraft continue to operate as multi-mission-capable and are available to undertake a wide range of assignments such as target aircraft for the Coast Guard's rotary-wing air-intercept training, flight-test operations, airborne-incident assessment, and operations in which general-aviation aircraft are valuable. AuxAir makes a viable supporting contribution to efforts against future terrorist attacks, and, in an era of high operating costs, it should be considered a significant and resilient, ready-responsive force multiplier.

AuxAir Mission Profile

The contribution made by small, general-aviation aircraft as observation platforms in World War II, Korea, and Vietnam remains important. The value of small planes should not be underestimated, especially when the focus is supporting the Coast Guard mission from the air. Of considerable benefit, Auxiliary aircraft, because of their variety of type, performance, and numbers, and because they are readily available, are highly adaptable and versatile platforms for deployment in the operational environment. The typical Auxiliary aircraft provides flexibility for mission-specific tasks including integrated operations with Coast Guard air, surface, and Auxiliary float and land mobile units and, when required, state and federal agencies.

AuxAir's mission profile now includes a closer relationship to those small liaison airplanes of the past: observation, reconnaissance, aerial photography, and now DHS and Maritime Domain Awareness missions. AuxAir units are commonly situated along the nation's coastlines, ports, and harbors, on top of major tributaries and larger inland lakes.

Coast Guard District 11, AuxAir Squadron 11N

Among the most prolific AuxAir programs in the country is Squadron 11N responsible for a considerable area of responsibility including the greater San Francisco Bay and two deepwater shipping channels connecting the port facilities of Sacramento and Stockton to the Bay Area. Of considerable concern are the complex labyrinths of the immense San Joaquin Delta region and its 1,200 miles of navigable waterways, which are dangerous most of the year.

This important region contains a vast, fragile network of earthen dikes that always cause concern about potential breach and flooding during winter storms. Littoral shipping and barge traffic along the coast of northern California are squadron missions that feature 30-to-50-mile offshore Maritime Domain Awareness and large-vessel photo missions.

Squadron aircraft are separated into single-engine for the San Francisco Bay and delta (they patrol along California's shoreline), and twins for long-range and offshore missions, logistics, crew training, and VIP transportation. On any patrol, squadron aircraft easily range 300 to 400 miles.

Currently the squadron boasts a complement of ten aircraft flying from five airports based between San Francisco and Sacramento, and a roster of more than 130 aviators from seven Auxiliary flotillas. Having aircraft based at five widely spaced airports allows for a rapid response throughout the area of responsibility.

Entry into the squadron begins with an air program orientation that outlines the AuxAir mission, training, and qualifications. Pilot applicants first train as observers before beginning their training and qualification. This follows national requirements, but much is focused on the district's mission and especially flying safely in the complex and busy airspace over the San Francisco Bay. Each year pilots fly standardized Coast Guard flight and search-and-rescue check rides, and each year aircraft facilities undergo inspection by the squadron's maintenance team.

In early 2004, the squadron took a close look at its operational capability and how that could be expanded into a more viable force structure. This resulted in the Air Education Training Course, directed at expanding operational capability, refresher training, and ensuring that everyone does everything the same way. These courses are held each year at Coast Guard Air Station Sacramento to maintain standardization, facilitate multi-mission capability and air-surface-ground interface, and refine operational procedures.

Expandable Force Capability

Almost daily changes in security, safety, and especially maritime activities increase our vulnerabilities offshore, in port and harbor, and inland. The Coast Guard is addressing these challenges. But ever-diminishing budgets, the service's Deepwater program, and modernization stretch the dollar. If these factors were not enough, the shrinking Arctic ice cap opens new maritime shipping routes that further impact our operational challenge. This becomes an issue in personnel and assets, in terms of present and future planning. The question is always: Should we react or respond?

As the Coast Guard mission increases in operation and reach, so too will its need for personnel and assets. Using Auxiliary capability conserves and releases regular service personnel and units for more hazardous or specialized operations. This makes the Auxiliary an immediately available resource for acquisition of personnel and equipment at a fraction of the cost.

Does this not suggest a broader, more expanded role for the Auxiliary? It would allow the organization's operational responsibilities to increase, while taking greater advantage of the service's personnel, capabilities, and available assets to complement the expanding mission requirement. Although Auxiliarists receive no salary—they are reimbursed for fuel and minimal maintenance—their satisfaction with serving alongside Coast Guard colleagues as "America's lifesavers" is compensation enough.

It seems only logical and operationally productive to expand the Auxiliary's role. With greater operational use of its average 35,000 members, 5,000 small boats, and 150 general-aviation aircraft, this integration of a diverse and responsive, cost-effective force multiplier clearly benefits both the Coast Guard and the nation.

5 "COAST GUARD DOGS FIGHT TERRORISM"

CAPT W. Russell Webster, USCG (Ret.)

Not to be forgotten as part of Team Coast Guard are man's best friend, U.S. Coast Guard dogs. Captain Webster does an outstanding job profiling the canines of the U.S. Coast Guard, which, after September 11, have homeland security missions in addition to their collateral duties as mascots. This is a good, light read about the four-legged members of Team Coast Guard.

"COAST GUARD DOGS FIGHT TERRORISM"

By CAPT W. Russell Webster, USCG (Ret.),
U.S. Naval Institute *Proceedings* (December 2004): 78.

Specially trained canine units patrolling busy U.S. ports are some of the Coast Guard's newest weapons in the twenty-first-century war on terrorism. Each year, U.S. ports host thousands of foreign-flag ships carrying multinational crews and cargoes from around the globe. Former Coast Guard Commandant Admiral James Loy noted that the 11 September 2001 attacks could have occurred at maritime facilities.

The key to successfully combating maritime terrorism is maritime domain awareness (MDA): complete knowledge of which ships are on the ocean and of the people and cargo aboard them. It enables law enforcement agencies to focus their scarce resources on specific vessels of interest. Ideally, MDA takes place as far away from U.S. waters as possible, even in foreign ports before ships depart for the United States. In some cases, however, the Coast Guard must board and inspect vessels in or just outside U.S. ports.

High-Interest Vessels

High-interest vessels (HIVs) generally are large foreign commercial vessels (600–1,100 feet long), often with all-foreign crewmembers. Law enforcement officials decide whether to board them depending on factors such as their flags of registry, crew nationalities, types of cargo, and last ports of call. Bostonians probably are most familiar with the large liquefied natural gas carriers that are HIVs. After the 11 September attacks, they were prohibited from entering the port of Boston until adequate security measures could be put in place. HIVs require differing levels of scrutiny by the Coast Guard, Immigration and Naturalization Service, Customs Service, and—oftentimes—counterpart agencies in other nations.

Dogs are especially useful for searching large HIVs (including cruise and container ships) because of the many sizeable areas where explosives, terrorists, and terrorist-related materials can be hidden. An incident in October 2001 demonstrated the possible threat. Egyptian Rizik Amid Farid was intercepted dockside in Gioia Tauro, Italy. Unlike most stowaways, he was smartly dressed and found living in a 40-foot cargo container. Farid's comfortable living accommodations included cell and satellite phones and a computer. He also had airport diagrams, credentials indicating he was an aircraft mechanic, a Canadian passport, and a one-way airline ticket to a foreign destination. Obviously, Farid carried documents and apparatuses that an illegal immigrant would have been unable to obtain or afford.

Dogs in Search & Security Roles

Dogs are not new to the Coast Guard or the port of Boston. During World War II, the service's Beach Patrol used 1,800 dogs to protect coastlines, ports, and harbors from German incursions and sabotage. The Coast Guard has renewed its interest in using them for homeland security because of their ability to substantially reduce the amount of time spent searching for suspicious people and cargo. In 2001, data indicated that less than 2% of the 6,000,000 shipping containers that entered the United States annually were inspected by law enforcement agencies.

As of this month, the Coast Guard has 19 dogs trained to detect explosives. Each canine will be paired with a human handler. Dogs and masters will bond by eating, sleeping, and training together for most of the animal's life. As in World War II, human-canine teams will be as efficient as two or more people (depending on circumstances) in searching HIVs and other large ships. Future applications could call for sending these teams out to search ships before they enter port.

Trained detector dog-handler teams are skillful at exposing explosives and other hazardous materials that terrorists may try to smuggle into U.S. ports in foreign trade ships. The dogs have proved their mettle in a number of situations and gained the reputation for great alertness and for being formidable attackers. According to one government study, a large dog, attacking with teeth bared, is often a more dangerous adversary than a man with a gun. Other government studies indicate that the dogs' security usefulness is increased significantly when an enemy's religious beliefs hold that canines are unholy and unclean. In such cases, the mere knowledge that the Coast Guard employs canines might dissuade would-be attackers of ships and critical facilities.

Dog-handler teams will be part of well-trained Maritime Safety and Security Teams (MSSTs), Coast Guard professionals who provide highly mobile boat forces and security elements for protecting ports. The MSSTs are billed as the Coast Guard's special forces, with teams based around the United States, including near Boston. They are rapid-response organizations that can deploy humans and canines within hours to distant locations for antiterrorism operations.

The Coast Guard has taken old tricks and updated them for the war on terrorism. Using canines as guards and detectors of stowaways and explosive materials may well prove more advantageous in this war than it was in the past.

6 "VIEW FROM THE BRIDGE"

RADM Gary T. Blore, USCG

After decades of chronic underfunding, the U.S. Coast Guard is in dire need of modernization. This March 2007 *Proceedings* article by Rear Admiral Gary Blore, USCG, explains the urgent need to modernize the Coast Guard's antique fleet of cutters, aircraft, and communication systems. Modernizing the USCG is a bargain according to Rear Admiral Blore—$24 billion over twenty-five years. It was unfortunate that the Coast Guard's important modernization program received a lot of unflattering press at the outset. Blore sets the record straight. This article is a good read indeed because a fully modernized USCG is vital to the national defense of the United States.

"VIEW FROM THE BRIDGE"

By RADM Gary T. Blore, USCG, U.S. Naval Institute *Proceedings* (March 2007): 68–72.

In the quarter-century span between 2002 and 2027, the U.S. Coast Guard will spend upward of $24 billion to modernize and replace its aging inventory of cutters, aircraft, and supporting systems. Five years into this effort—commonly known as the Deepwater Program—we find ourselves the subject of intense scrutiny from Congress and, perhaps more surprising for an agency renowned for its thriftiness, at the center of some sensational news stories warning of the fleecing of America.

Without doubt, the program has sometimes fallen short of expectations. Some of the criticism printed "above the fold" in the mainstream press and elsewhere has been deserved and has caused us to take a serious look at what we can do better. Some of the coverage, though, has been rather wide of the mark and a certain amount of it, just plain wrong. Because of this, many readers haven't had the necessary context or facts to meaningfully assess the program's effectiveness.

As radio commentator Paul Harvey is fond of saying, having "the rest of the story" leads to fuller understanding of Deepwater's challenges and its achievements. Here are two examples where having "the rest of the story" really matters:

First, it has been reported that costs for the program have grown from $17 billion to $24 billion. This is true, but there's a reasonable explanation for the change. The original Deepwater implementation plan was developed before the tragedy that occurred on 11 September 2001. Following the service's transfer to the Department of Homeland Security in March 2003, we conducted a performance gap analysis, drafted a new mission needs statement, and revised our implementation plan to ensure Deepwater capabilities would support enhanced mission emphasis newly assigned to the Coast Guard; e.g., maritime homeland security. All of these steps were carried out in full consultation with the Bush administration and Congress, who committed to this level of investment. The increased costs can thus largely be attributed to a considered decision to increase capabilities and not to cost overruns, as some have suggested.

Second, it's not readily apparent from most recent coverage that the program has had any success at all, yet dozens of Deepwater assets are already operating in the fleet and making a difference today. A climber who fell down the side of a mountain last July in the Olympic National Forest owes his life to a daring rescue executed by a well-trained air crew from Coast Guard Air Station Port Angeles, Washington. What's the connection? The rescuers were flying a recently delivered HH-65C helicopter, newly re-engined as part of the

Deepwater Program. So far, more than 80 B model HH-65s have been converted to Cs, giving them the ability to carry greater loads and remain aloft for longer periods. Had the climber fallen just two weeks earlier—before the station's Charlies were delivered—the rescue would not have been attempted and the outcome would have been very different. Also, sensor and communications equipment upgrades on 39 cutters are directly contributing to the execution of Coast Guard missions worldwide and also facilitate seamless operations with the U.S. Navy.

Fifteen major acquisition projects are currently under way within the Deepwater Program, underscoring its complexity. Imagine the challenges the Navy and U.S. Marine Corps would face if they assigned their top 15 projects to one office. Yet historical circumstances drove the Coast Guard to do exactly that. Here's why.

By the end of the 1990s, most of the Coast Guard's ships and aircraft were at or approaching the end of their service lives. In 1997, the chairman of the Navy League's Coast Guard Affairs Committee exhorted readers of *Sea Power* magazine to launch a rescue mission for the Coast Guard, noting: "The Coast Guard's capital plant has a value of approximately $19 billion. Based on industry standards—annual replacement of 5 percent of capital assets—the Coast Guard's average acquisition, construction, and improvement expenditures should be $950 million, but actually have been under $200 million, in constant dollars, over the past 20 years."

Forced to Act

This perennial underfunding for capital investments had resulted in imminent block obsolescence, and the service was forced to act immediately to ensure it could continue to save lives, defend 95,000 miles of American coastline, protect natural resources, and support the nation's economy by ensuring the free flow of U.S. trade by sea.

Given the massive task at hand, a traditional, piecemeal replacement of failing assets didn't seem to make much sense. Therefore, we determined it would be more cost-effective and efficient to adopt a mission-based performance approach to acquiring an integrated system of assets—referred to as a "system of systems"—to give the service functional capabilities to perform missions worldwide. With respect to our unique approach, the General Accounting Office, now the Government Accountability Office (GAO), in 1998 concluded: "The (Coast Guard's) 'system of systems' approach seems logical as a way to avoid a costly one-for-one replacement of assets."

Originally called the Deepwater Capability Replacement Project, the program was established formally in 1996, following extensive needs analysis, and the Coast Guard developed an acquisition strategy to support the project. In alignment with the Government Performance Results Act, OMB Circular A-109, and other government-wide acquisition reform legislation and regulations, the Deepwater strategy incorporated insights and recommendations from the GAO, the Department of Transportation Office of the Inspector General (OIG), and other independent experts.

The Coast Guard recognized that after years of slim procurement budgets, our cadre of in-house acquisition professionals required greater capacity to harmonize the execution of Deepwater's comprehensive recapitalization program. In what has turned out to be one of the most often discussed aspects of the program, a decision was made to employ from industry a single systems integrator with experience in managing Level I acquisitions, which are large-scale projects in the general cost range of more than $250 million. In selecting our systems integration team from industry, the Coast Guard put primary emphasis on achieving a comprehensive, integrated solution for Deepwater because we believed such a solution would lead to synergies and efficiencies. Following full and open competition, the contract for the Integrated Deepwater System was awarded in 2002 to Integrated Coast Guard Systems, a joint venture of Lockheed Martin and Northrop Grumman.

Nobody ever said recapitalizing the fleet would be easy. Reports from the GAO, OIG, and an array of independent third parties stated that in spite of "excellent" planning it would be hard—really hard—to obtain adequate funding and staffing and provide appropriate levels of oversight to contractors. A team of experts from Acquisition Solutions, Inc., (ASI) perhaps summed it up best in its review of the program, saying: "First, risk is part of every acquisition. There will always be significant cost, schedule, and performance risks inherent in projects of this size, scope, and complexity. Second, outsourcing a difficult task does not make it any easier. The Coast Guard still must identify existing, potential, and emerging risks and develop measures to mitigate and manage the risks." And, in an echo of the Navy League's earlier appeal for support to modernize the fleet, ASI continued: "Third, this is a mission-essential, unavoidable requirement and major investment is inevitable."

Our initial projections set the Deepwater budget at $300 million for the first year, and $500 million for each year thereafter. Some believed the projected funding levels were unattainable and even then only minimally reflected necessary costs. Fortunately, thanks to bipartisan support from Congress, our program funding has increased every year since 2002. We received the program's first $1 billion annual appropriation in 2007. However, we don't take this support for granted and cost control remains foremost in our minds as we take the program into its second five years. Notwithstanding empirical knowledge that rising costs are an economic fact in shipbuilding, the Coast Guard, along with the Navy and industry, has pledged to reduce shipbuilding and other costs wherever possible.

Headwinds

Nevertheless, we have encountered other headwinds that have pushed back against our initial vision and projections of Deepwater's acquisition strategy. For example, a planned conversion of 49 patrol boats from 110 feet to 123 feet—our first project out of the chute—was halted after just eight conversions because of technical problems. Much has been written elsewhere about this disappointing episode, with no need to belabor it here. However, it should be noted that we only attempted such an unorthodox upgrade in the first place because projected budget constraints informed us we could not afford to recapitalize all of our platforms under Deepwater. We realized that choices and trade-offs had to be made, and modernizing our patrol boat fleet through the conversion was one of them. Even now, in light of the hard lessons we have learned through this project, a cross-functional team continues to study our problems with this conversion. The bottom line is that the Coast Guard's leadership is wholly committed to preventing future such occurrences.

Meanwhile, we have had to develop an interim solution to get patrol boats into the fleet as quickly as possible, after early tank testing showed technical risks with the initial composite hull design for our Fast Response Cutter. We're now working to acquire a "parent craft" design based on a vessel already in operation that will require minimal modifications to meet our basic mission requirements.

A recent report by the Department of Homeland Security OIG highlighted concerns with our approach to resolving potential hull fatigue-life issues on our National Security Cutter, the largest of Deepwater's three major classes of cutters. The Coast Guard hasn't built a ship on this scale for 35 years, so we didn't expect entirely smooth sailing. It is not uncommon for first-in-class ships such as the *Bertholf* (NSC-1) to experience some turbulence during design and construction. Nearly every ship the United States has built has encountered challenges and cost growth.

During design review and early construction, the Coast Guard incorporated many changes recommended by the then–chief engineer of the Coast Guard. However, further review of the cutter's design indicated the ship might also experience higher stress levels than anticipated, raising a question of the hull's fatigue life over the course of the cutter's 30-year service life. We have been addressing these concerns for several years now—in fact, had begun to address them long before the Inspector General's auditors arrived on the scene in the summer of 2005—and there has never been a question of safety related to the ship's structure or its ability to complete all assigned missions.

In collaboration with the Coast Guard's current chief engineer, who serves as the program's technical authority, and ICGS, we have developed structural enhancements that will be incorporated into the design of the cutters not yet under construction (hulls 3 through 8) and retrofitted into the first two currently being built.

Lessons Learned

Without question, the Coast Guard has collected a lengthy list of "lessons learned" about program and contract management and execution. ASI was right: outsourcing systems integration didn't make it easy. Although we're convinced the fundamental system of systems concept remains sound, we are adapting our vision for this acquisition program in light of experience. Our approach to Deepwater is evolving as the Coast Guard confronts, forthrightly, the challenges of building budgets under incremental funding profiles, post–9/11 mission requirements, and a Coast Guard acquisition culture that naturally prefers a more hands-on approach to its relationship with industry. We are learning that our original, less-structured approach to system integration must be tempered with stronger oversight and closer partnership ("trust but verify") with our partners in Integrated Coast Guard Systems.

It is prudent to keep in mind that we're in the early stages of what Congress has helped to define as a very long acquisition effort that will continue to evolve as the nation refines its maritime security strategy. Our original vision was a comprehensive program that would feature "one-stop shopping" for modernization and recapitalization. The program was to have demonstrated value added through reduced costs, using largely mature platforms and systems designs and commercial practices.

The reality of Deepwater today is that the Coast Guard has become more involved as a system integrator than we anticipated. The functionality of our Deepwater integrated product team model with industry has proved to be more complex in execution than our early due diligence indicated. Experience has taught us that the government and industry team must redouble its efforts to focus on total ownership cost management and maintaining focus on technical performance and program schedule.

While the challenges we face are formidable, every member of our Deepwater team knows that each day the Coast Guard embarks on dangerous missions in hostile and unforgiving environments. Our men and women require the enhanced capabilities promised by Deepwater. Simply put, the nation's maritime security and the safety of our citizens depend on our success, and we shall not fail to deliver.

The Coast Guard has recognized that Deepwater is entering a new and important phase in its evolution as a program. We have moved past the era of making our case as to why Deepwater is necessary; now we must focus on our commitment to excellence in executing this program. We must demonstrate our willingness to draw on the best practices of a broad cross-section of government and industry acquisition expertise. Under the leadership of our Commandant, Admiral Thad Allen, the service is aggressively implementing a series of improvements in program management to ensure effective oversight, sound stewardship of taxpayer dollars, and timely delivery of these much-awaited assets. Building on the GAO Framework for Acquisition Management, improvements already initiated or completed include:

- Consolidation of Coast Guard acquisition activities (Deepwater, Office of Acquisition, acquisition policy, and the Research and Development Center) into one directorate to increase efficiency and maximize human capital;
- Adoption of a DoD 5000-based revision to the Coast Guard's Major System Acquisition policies;
- Development of new evaluation criteria for the follow-on Deepwater contract term, beginning in June 2007;
- Renewed focus on hiring, certification, and retention of qualified contracting officers and program management personnel; and
- Increased government staffing at Deepwater manufacturing facilities to focus on quality assurance.

Independent Analyses

In addition, the Coast Guard is committed to independent, third-party analyses of our program, including technical assessments of all new, or principally new, asset designs, such as the Fast Response Cutter (A-class), for which we also recently completed an expanded business case analysis. Last fall, we contracted with the Defense Acquisition University for a "quick look" review to examine the program's key management and technical processes, performance-based acquisition strategy, organizational structure, and our government and industry partnership contract, as well as a study being conducted by the Coast Guard Research and Development Center to provide recommendations for the way ahead on the planned Deepwater Vertical-Launch Unmanned Aerial Vehicle (VUAV).

We believe these important first steps demonstrate our willingness to learn from our experience and to frankly assess our program's strengths and weaknesses. These measures also put us firmly on the path to correcting problems and to building the solutions that will deliver the next generation of capability to the fleet. However, it is the nature of any large acquisition effort that improvements in program management may not be evident for months or even years. Nevertheless, we are confident that, over time, these improvements in our processes and procedures will help us grow into the model, mid-sized federal acquisition entity we know we must become to meet expectations and deliver assets affordably and on schedule.

While we know we owe a debt of gratitude to the Coast Guard, departmental, and congressional leaders who had the vision to initiate the Deepwater Capability Replacement Project, we in Deepwater's second generation must recognize the confidence they placed in us to adjust the acquisition strategy based on lessons learned, funding realities, and current events. It is our duty to realize the program's original promise by recapitalizing the Coast Guard while integrating best practices resulting from both the past challenges, and current successes, of the Deepwater Program.

Editor's Note

The following three notes appeared with the original article.

Notes

1. James H. Thach III, *Sea Power*: Letters, May 1997.
2. GAO Report to the Subcommittee on Transportation, Committee on Appropriations, U.S. Senate (GAO/RCED-99–6), October 1998.
3. Independent Assessment of the United States Coast Guard "Integrated Deepwater System" Acquisition Issue Brief, July 2001.

7 "R&D CENTER DELIVERS BIG PUNCH"

CAPT Dennis Evans, USCG; LCDR Samuel Nassar, USCG; LT Keely Higbie, USCG; and Dr. Joe DiRenzo III

According to the USCG's official website, "The Research and Development Center, located in New London, Connecticut, is the Coast Guard's sole facility performing research, development, test, and evaluation in support of the service's major missions." Moreover, "The RDC is responsible for evaluating the feasibility and affordability of mission execution solutions and providing operational and risk-management analysis at all stages of the acquisition process." Yet it is one of the best-kept secrets in the entire USCG.

The authors of this August 2016 *Proceedings* article about the USCG's R&D Center did a great job in demonstrating the relevance of the R&D Center to the rest of the USCG. They were right on target when they wrote, "The Coast Guard R&D program has been a significant force multiplier for the strategic, operational, and tactical levels of the service."

"R&D CENTER DELIVERS BIG PUNCH"

By CAPT Dennis Evans, USCG; LCDR Samuel Nassar, USCG;
LT Keely Higbie, USCG; and Dr. Joe DiRenzo III,

U.S. Naval Institute *Proceedings* (August 2016): 38–44.

Discussions on research and development (R&D) can vary based on the audience. Some may think of modern tech startups that research app development or new ways to engage across social media. Others picture a sterile work environment where breakthrough medications are created, improved, and tested. And of course, there may be those who imagine high-tech labs inventing state-of-the-art gadgets and machines. All these images are accurate, as are many more. R&D is one means by which an organization can grow and adapt, and governments, industries, and other organizations are constantly investigating and researching with the aim of making a discovery that can lead to either the development or the improvement of new tactics, technology, and procedures.

The Coast Guard R&D program has been a significant force multiplier for the strategic, operational, and tactical levels of the service. From developing more effective ways to conduct operations to looking for new systems to address growing issues within the Maritime Transportation System, Coast Guard R&D has been an agile capability within the service. At any given time, the program is working on more than 70 projects that support Coast Guard requirements across all mission areas, pursuing technologies that provide incremental improvements as well as those with the greatest potential to strategically transform the way the Coast Guard does business.

The program also leverages partnerships with academia, other government agencies, and private industry to anticipate and research solutions to future technological challenges. Partners include the Department of Homeland Security (DHS), university-based Centers of Excellence, national labs such as the Oak Ridge and Pacific Northwest National Labs, and private industry.

Focusing not only on traditional Coast Guard missions such as search and rescue and oil pollution response but also emerging threats such as cyber security, the service's R&D program has had multiple successes based on an understanding of national strategies and operational needs.

Little-Known Successes, Big Impact

The Coast Guard Research and Development Center (RDC) is the sole facility in the Coast Guard performing research, development, test, and evaluation (RDT&E) that supports the service's 11 statutory missions. Return on investment is a key element of every project, and that "return" can take many forms, ranging from creating more effective, efficient, and focused operations to offering options to decision makers on courses of action. Since its inception, the RDC has had a string of successes; however, these have not always received broad visibility within the Coast Guard. In addition, although the impact on the maritime public is significant, few Americans know about these good-news stories.

For example, during the mid-1970s the RDC developed an oil identification system (OIS) that can distinguish the unique properties of oils and determine if a relationship exists between samples of spilled oil and a suspected source. OIS has enabled the Coast Guard to identify sources of oil that have been illegally dumped into the ocean, resulting in accountability and prosecution of offenders.

The RDC also developed the visual and sensor "sweep width tables" used in the Search-and-Rescue Optimal Planning System (SAROPS). SAROPS is a software program all Coast Guard command centers use to develop search planning. The RDC recently expanded the program to include the unique requirements inherent in ice searches, which, if successful, will enhance an air crew's ability to conduct rescues in areas such as the Arctic. This will give the responding Coast Guard assets better tools to find and rescue people in the water, where every second is precious.

The RDC also is able to provide senior leaders unbiased, academically rigorous analysis that can be used as a part of the strategic decision-making process. The Center was at the forefront of analysis of unmanned aircraft systems for the national security cutter. Its alternatives analysis underscored that, based on requirements, a proposed vertical takeoff and landing platform would not be the right fit, avoiding more than $1 billion in prospective acquisitions.

In addition, the RDC collaborated with the DHS Science and Technology Center of Excellence at the University of Southern California to develop the Port Resilience Operational Tactical Enforcement Counter Terrorism (PROTECT) project. This was the first widely accepted use of game theory in port, waterways, and coastal security (PWCS) mission planning, and spawned changes to the *Maritime Security Response Operations Manual*. By changing times, locations, and activities of individual patrols, PROTECT inserts an element of uncertainty in an adversary's decision-making chain, while also introducing an element of deterrence. Similar in approach to community-oriented policing that concentrates on areas with highest risk while varying activities and engagement, PROTECT was a springboard to greater randomization of security activities within a port. The operational impact is an increased Coast Guard on-the-water presence, which the general public has noticed. To quote a water-taxi operator in Boston, "I have been in this harbor for a few years. Lately I see you guys all the time. . . . Where did you get all the boats?"

These success stories are part of a larger narrative in which the RDC's research leads to innovation that directly affects operations. Investment in the RDC helps shape Coast Guard operations.

Support to Western Hemisphere Strategy

The *U.S. Coast Guard Western Hemisphere Strategy* confronts challenges in the United States' most important geographic theater of operations, to include combating criminal networks, securing U.S. borders, safeguarding commerce, and building partner-nation capacity. To support this strategy, the RDC is exploring applications of small unmanned aircraft systems to increase offshore presence by enhancing surveillance capability and reach from cutters and small boats. In addition, probabilistic-based search models are being explored to improve patrol tactics in a given geographic area. The output from these models incorporates optimal tactics assuming that the adversary will adapt when reaching a certain threshold of failure. The primary objective is to analyze the findings derived from modeling and simulation runs to better understand the adversary's tactical shifts and leading indicators so Coast Guard operational commanders can improve the efficiency and effectiveness of their interdiction mission patrols. Follow-on research will determine whether adjustments to equipment and asset capabilities and/or capacity might be needed.

A COAST GUARD RDC SEA STORY

During the 1940s, pigeons in a Tufts University laboratory demonstrated the exceptional ability to pick out certain shapes and colors in exchange for food. In the late 1970s and early 1980s, the Coast Guard decided this ability could be useful in searching for persons and equipment in open water. In Project Sea Hunt, Navy scientist Dr. Jim Simmons trained pigeons to conduct search-and-rescue missions from Coast Guard helicopters.

Three pigeons in a small observation bubble on the underside of a helicopter were positioned so they covered the 360 degrees under the aircraft. The pigeons were trained to recognize objects floating in the water and to communicate with the helicopter pilots by pecking a key that would help guide the pilots to the targets. The birds were 93 percent accurate at locating objects floating at sea—human flight crews were accurate 38 percent of the time—and their false positive rates were extremely low. When combined with human searchers, the success rate was nearly perfect. Eventually, the Coast Guard recognized the value of Simmons' pigeons and called this project "the best daylight search system" yet developed.

Unfortunately, two helicopters crashed, which either destroyed or damaged the pigeon system. Project Sea Hunt never got out of the testing phase and was ended in 1983 because of federal budget cuts. Though innovative in theory, the project ultimately proved impractical.

The RDC's efforts supporting search-and-rescue missions continued, however, and in 2015 the RDC tested an electronic sensor system on board H-60 and H-65 helicopters. This forward-looking infrared radar (FLIR) ball provided a similar capability to that of the pigeons, as its sensors could detect differences in light and contrast not easily seen by the human eye.

As planners look at the results, they will be able to determine the optimal asset mix. This information, coupled with queued intelligence, presents a formidable capability to address narcotics and human smuggling and will enable the Coast Guard to position assets where they can best effect interdictions. In many ways the RDC's efforts channel Sun Tzu's belief: "When we are able to attack, we must seem unable; when using our forces, we must appear inactive; when we are near, we must make the enemy believe we are far away; when far away, we must make him believe we are near."

The RDC continues to develop and maintain the Coast Guard Maritime Operational Effectiveness Simulation (CGMOES) application. This initiative addresses the need for an easy-to-use, streamlined capability for routine Coast Guard-wide asset allocation and force-structure decision support. The project's objectives include providing quick answers to senior leaders' force-structure questions driven by Congress regarding eliminations and additions of asset classes, as well as changes in mission priorities. CGMOES support to Coast Guard fleet acquisition programs yields the most impact. Currently, the RDC is providing the Commandant with the results of the RDC's Fleet Mix Analysis study to inform the multibillion-dollar offshore patrol cutter acquisition, one of the largest potential acquisitions in the service's history. In terms of its return on investment, CGMOES significantly improves the Coast Guard's ability to conduct trade studies to support acquisition efforts and assists operational commanders with strategic force lay-down options.

Cyber Strategy in the Maritime Domain

The *U.S. Coast Guard Cyber Strategy* aims to strengthen the cybersecurity of the nation's maritime domain and further develop a robust internal cybersecurity capability. In support of this strategy, the RDC is developing a conceptual framework and visualization tool that can accept sourced command, control, communications, computers, and information technology (C4IT) component data (hardware, firmware, and software) to more quickly and effectively assess the Coast Guard's cybersecurity posture.

The RDC also is undertaking cybersecurity initiatives that support the Maritime Transportation System. Efforts in this area are helping to establish a sound framework of cybersecurity documentation, procedures, and tools in support of maritime critical infrastructure. Specific work includes analysis of cybersecurity documentation tools, an assessment of port-facility network vulnerabilities, and an analysis of supervisory control and data acquisition and integrated control system vulnerabilities.

In addition, the RDC is leveraging both DHS Centers of Excellence and other major universities to advance maritime cyber research. Recently, the Coast Guard's deputy commandant for operations selected three research areas for the American Military University, Rutgers University, and the University of Southern California to address: developing maritime cybersecurity information-sharing protocols to meet the needs of industry and government, exploring how best to promote the use of sound cyber risk-management principles in the maritime domain, and researching threats and vulnerabilities modeling to better understand maritime cyber. The results of these efforts were scheduled to be briefed in late July. The second phase of this initiative will explore new research topics involving maritime cyber. The RDC's collective effort on cybersecurity is a return on investment not only for the service but also for elements of the Maritime Transportation System. Moreover, engagement with multiple university partners highlights forward-leaning research to address the service's needs through new thinking infused with academic rigor.

Arctic Operations

The *U.S. Coast Guard Arctic Strategy* has three goals: to increase domain awareness, improve governance structure and capabilities, and broaden partnerships necessitated by the Arctic's growing maritime usage. To support this strategy, the Coast Guard called on the RDC to conduct a high-latitude study of future Coast Guard mission and resource requirements in this new priority operational area. This study has become the foundation for a variety of Arctic initiatives, strategy, and the major acquisition of new 21st-century capabilities (i.e., polar icebreakers) for this emerging region of the U.S. exclusive economic zone.

The RDC has orchestrated a number of efforts to demonstrate and evaluate technologies and methods to enhance Coast Guard mission performance in the remote and harsh Arctic environment. This includes evaluating various unmanned systems' capabilities to detect, monitor, and track oil spills for response, as well as teaming manned and unmanned systems in support of search-and-rescue operations. "The Arctic technology evaluations provide [the Coast Guard] with the synergy of working with the researchers and learning which ways they need to reach out to the Alaskan native communities as they research what really impacts those local people here," explained Sudie Hargis, the tribal liaison for Coast Guard District 17.

The RDC also completed modeling predictions to determine Coast Guard communication coverage using high-frequency radio throughout the Arctic region. The modeling results highlighted how the radio frequency propagation of the Arctic affects range, clarity, and consistency over time. Field-based experiments using new and existing satellite options such as the Department of Defense's Mobile User Objective System and Distributed Tactical Communications System, as well as experiments with new antennas, were conducted in various inland locations to identify ways to improve connectivity.

The Arctic Navigational Safety Information System (ANSIS) functional design project established a mutually agreed-upon design of the prototype system for near-shore ANSIS, which has the potential to enhance mariners' capability to identify, assess, and mitigate navigational risks and to improve the Coast Guard's maritime domain awareness in the Arctic region. The RDC established a three-year, renewable cooperative R&D agreement with the Marine Exchange of Alaska to define, develop, test, install, and monitor a next-generation navigational safety information system for the Arctic.

Energy Renaissance Action Plan Support

The Coast Guard's *Energy Renaissance Action Plan* guides the service in ensuring the maritime safety, security, and stewardship of U.S. energy production and transport by focusing on incident prevention, preparedness, and response capabilities. To support this action plan, the RDC is implementing and analyzing a 21st-century electronic navigation technology (e-Nav) that takes advantage of electronic data systems, communications, and navigation capabilities, making it less reliant on physical aids. e-Nav technology will be set up and operated along a section of the Western Rivers system, and electronic aids to navigation (e-AtoN) and electronic maritime safety information (e-MSI) will be provided to mariners in a test area. This effort will provide the Coast Guard, Army Corps of Engineers, and other partners with experience in distributing navigation information to users through the Automatic Identification System (AIS). The project's outcome will inform the development of Coast Guard policy and authority requirements for delivering information to support safe navigation, a core Coast Guard mission. This effort will decrease the number of buoys the Coast Guard maintains and increase transparency on U.S. waterways.

As part of its effort to detect and mitigate oil within the water column, the RDC partnered with the Bureau of Safety and Environmental Enforcement to find and remove oil down to 10,000 feet. The first part of the effort focused on the development of detection systems to identify and track subsurface oil spills. The partners developed and tested two prototypes (optical and sonar) that can detect small droplets of oil at high resolution in all environmental conditions—offshore, near shore, and in rivers—and mark subsurface oil for possible removal. The next phase of the project will focus on developing a technology, technique, or strategy to reduce the impact of oil within the water column on the surrounding environment and/or manmade structures. The mitigation prototype testing and concept development will provide the Coast Guard and its partners with improved operational performance and resilient response execution.

On the response front, the RDC's mobile technology research is improving the collection and integration of information during large-scale "incidents of national significance," such as a major oil spill. Combining tablet technology with a mobile ad hoc network, the RDC continues to refine ways to facilitate response and coordinate multiple crews covering different areas and tasked with different jobs during large-scale incidents. What is the return on investment? The California Office of Emergency Services is using this technology now with great results. The RDC continues to explore and evaluate this capability with DHS first responders and Massachusetts Institute of Technology Lincoln Laboratories. This research will provide responders and decision makers with the timeliest, fused information readily available.

Turning Research into Innovation

Each of these projects comes to the RDC from operators in the Coast Guard. The RDC solicits research ideas from all levels of the organization. With the Coast Guard's 11 statutory missions as guidance, these ideas serve as the primary vehicles for project creation and innovation. Once received, ideas are formally reviewed, prioritized by Coast Guard needs and requirements' owners, and developed into executable project plans.

The true strengths of the RDC's testing efforts are found in the field. The RDC considers the field to be its lab space, and much of its most effective test and evaluation work is performed on board operational Coast Guard assets. During project development, test, and evaluation, the RDC works with the Coast Guard's Atlantic Area (LANTAREA) and Pacific Area (PACAREA) within the service's standard operational planning process (SOPP) to identify assets—including cutters, boats, aircraft, and subject matter experts—to support field activities. The SOPP is the formal methodology the service uses to assign assets to missions.

Five years ago, the RDC began integrating its asset requests into the operational planning document development and request-for-forces processes. Through dedicated engagement with LANTAREA and PACAREA, assets quickly are identified to field-test new technology, techniques, tactics, and procedures. This ongoing engagement has benefited both research and operations—the RDC understands the constraints operators are under, and the operators see and experience firsthand how the RDT&E program supports tactical operations. The RDC currently is using Coast Guard assets to test new investigative tools to locate and prosecute search-and-rescue hoax call violators. The feedback from operators is vital, especially as the goal is to transition projects into implementation in the fleet.

An Evolving Asset

Since its inception, the RDC has been a valuable and agile asset to the Coast Guard. In the 1970s and early 1980s, the RDC focused on modernizing the service's aids-to-navigation and search-and-rescue capabilities. Supporting these missions continues to be an important part of the RDC portfolio. In the 1980s and 1990s, several high-profile oil spills resulted in spill response becoming a major research area. In the late 1990s and the 2000s, the RDC shifted its focus to support cutter acquisitions and to improve the efficiency of a wide range of Coast Guard operations. Following the attacks of 11 September 2001, military and civilian RDC personnel provided staffing, expertise, and a big-picture look at homeland defense. Since then, the RDC has pursued new products that will assist the Coast Guard in protecting U.S. ports and enhancing homeland security.

During the 2010 Deepwater Horizon oil spill, the RDC quickly stood up an independent analysis and technology assessment program to provide technical assistance to the incident command on the evaluation of specific emergent technologies and the thousands of ideas received from the general public. The RDC's contributions earned the RDT&E Program the Coast Guard Commander Joel Magnussen Innovation Award for Management in 2011.

The Coast Guard's mission set always is evolving, and the RDC plays a critical role in ensuring the Coast Guard can continue to effectively and efficiently perform its services to the American people. The RDC has pushed the boundaries, working with multiple elements within DHS, with Coast Guard partners, and in the Coast Guard to ensure the deck-plate level operators are prepared for this evolution. The unit's command emblem includes its motto, which represents the heart of the RDC: "From here, you can see tomorrow."

8 "IF WE DIDN'T HAVE A COAST GUARD WE'D HAVE TO BUILD ONE"

Hon. Mortimer L. Downey

The 1999 Interagency Task Force on U.S. Coast Guard Roles and Missions was a vital milestone in the USCG's modernization program. It was no secret that the USCG's cutters, aircraft, and communication systems all needed to be replaced. Yet, as often is the case with the bureaucracy in Washington, D.C., nothing bold such as a fully modernized USCG will be pursued until after a commission of experts is formed and issues a report. This USCG commission was no different.

Deputy Secretary of Transportation Mortimer L. Downey previewed the commission's report, entitled "A Coast Guard for the Twenty-First Century," in this December 1999 *Proceedings* article. This report was prescient on the USCG's roles and missions given the terrorist attacks on 9/11 and the Coast Guard's response ever since to protect the United States from another terrorist attack in our ports and waterways as well as on the high seas.

"IF WE DIDN'T HAVE A COAST GUARD WE'D HAVE TO BUILD ONE"

By Hon. Mortimer L. Downey, U.S. Naval Institute *Proceedings* (December 2000): 32–34.

As the United States looked to a new millennium, the time was ripe to look at the Coast Guard's future. But before we could chart a new course for the service, we had to answer some difficult questions. What are the nature and scope of the threats and challenges facing the nation on its maritime borders and inland waterways? What is the best course of action to deal with them? If the U.S. Coast Guard did not exist, would we have to invent it? If we determined that the nation needed a first-rate coast guard, what roles and missions should it perform, and what would it need to carry them out safely and affordably?

Such questions and uncertainties convinced President Bill Clinton in March 1999 to establish the Interagency Task Force on U.S. Coast Guard Roles and Missions, with a mandate to "provide advice and recommendations regarding the appropriate roles and missions for the United States Coast Guard through the year 2020." After nearly a year of intensive study, interviews, meetings, and briefings, the task force was unanimous in its key findings:

- The United States has the world's best coast guard.
- The nation confronts numerous threats and challenges, in its inland and coastal waters, territorial seas, and exclusive economic zones, as well as on the high seas.
- The Coast Guard has compelling roles and missions in five critical areas: maritime security, national defense, protection of natural resources, maritime safety, and maritime mobility.
- Significant investments, particularly in the service's "deepwater" operating environment, are needed to guarantee the U.S. Coast Guard will remain capable of meeting the demands that will be thrust on it.

The Coast Guard of the 21st Century

The task force's December 1999 report, "A Coast Guard for the Twenty-First Century," outlines the results of our deliberations.[1] Most fundamentally, we are convinced the Coast Guard provides the United States a broad range of vital services that will be increasingly important in the decades ahead. In addition, we are unanimous in our affirmation of Coast Guard capabilities as a national priority, and we strongly recommend that the nation take action soon to modernize and recapitalize Coast Guard forces.

The task force members, drawn from 16 executive-branch stakeholder agencies and entities that compete for a constrained federal budget, found it in the vital interest of the nation to fully support the Coast Guard. We reached six overarching conclusions that underscore the importance of the Coast Guard, its roles and missions, and the support it requires to continue to meet the nation's needs through 2020. These are:

1. *The Coast Guard's roles and missions support national policies and objectives that will endure into the 21st century.* Our nation's future is being shaped by globally linked economies, revolutions in maritime transportation and information systems, emerging threats to the marine environment, and expanding concepts of national security. Thus, the federal government has a legitimate and abiding interest in maintaining the Coast Guard's active presence and effective influence in the nation's inland and coastal waters and on the high seas.
2. *The United States will continue to need a flexible, adaptable, multimission, military Coast Guard to meet national maritime interests and requirements well into the next century.* The Coast Guard's people and assets, by which national policies are implemented, are a unified whole—a singular, integrated, synergistic system of boats, cutters, aircraft, and command, control, communications, computer, intelligence, surveillance, and reconnaissance (C^4ISR) systems that has capabilities and usefulness across a broad range of civil and military missions. This

multimission capability makes the Coast Guard one of the most efficient agencies in government. Overall national policy must preserve the Coast Guard's adaptability, mission flexibility, and efficiency.

3. *To hedge against tomorrow's uncertainties, the Coast Guard should be rebuilt so as to be adaptable to future realities.* The Coast Guard of the future must have the flexibility to respond to a wide range of maritime threats and challenges—a fact that must be reflected in today's planning for tomorrow's systems, forces, and operations. National policy for the Coast Guard and today's capitalization decisions must enable tomorrow's Coast Guard to address current as well as unknown future realities.
4. *The Coast Guard should continue to pursue new methods and technologies to enhance its ability to perform its missions.* The Coast Guard is or will be reviewing its internal procedures, platforms, and systems in the near future. Review of intelligence-related issues is a necessary input to planning the Integrated Deepwater Capabilities Replacement Project's C^4 requirements.[2] And other issues, such as the ability to operate with other civilian agencies and military services, will be addressed as part of the Coast Guard's efforts to update its doctrine, management structure, and processes.
5. *Recapitalization of the Coast Guard's deepwater capability is a near-term national priority.* Modernization of the Coast Guard's deepwater assets is the key means for ensuring essential and sustained Coast Guard performance. The Coast Guard's deepwater cutters, aircraft, and C^4ISR assets are nearing the ends of their useful service lives. Therefore, planning for modernizing and replacing these capabilities must continue apace.
6. *The Deepwater Project is a sound approach to that end and the Interagency Task Force strongly endorses its process and timeline.* The Coast Guard has asked industry for conceptual approaches to maximize system effectiveness and minimize system cost by building new assets, refurbishing existing platforms, or transferring other agencies' excess assets. The

Deepwater Project's strategy and method are worthy of both investment and strong multiagency support and the project should move forward expeditiously and without interruption.

In addition to these six conclusions, the task force confirmed the importance of the Coast Guard in meeting numerous national and maritime security needs:

- Alien migrant interdiction and enforcement of U.S. immigration laws at sea
- Reducing the maritime flow of illicit narcotics into the United States
- Conducting national defense missions and specialized missions as assigned; acting as a force-in-being, ready and equipped to perform complementary duties in support of the Navy
- Preserving and protecting the nation's living marine resources in its exclusive economic zones and on the high seas; enforcing U.S. resource laws and regulations at sea
- Protecting our nation's marine environment through enforcement of environmental laws at sea and prevention of and response to oil and hazardous chemical spills
- Ensuring maritime safety
- Protecting and maintaining our nation's ports and waterways
- Providing public services in the most efficient manner possible
- Providing a cost-effective and integrated system of cutters, aircraft, sensors, and support systems to meet the nation's maritime security needs

Roles & Missions and the Deepwater Project

The Coast Guard's roles and missions will continue to support national policies and objectives well into the 21st century, but existing Coast Guard assets will not meet the service's mission requirements through the next 20 years. Indeed, the service's inventory of deepwater cutters, aircraft, and C^4ISR systems is aging; today's assets are technologically and operationally obsolete.

Figure 1. COAST GUARD STRATEGIC PERFORMANCE GOALS

MARITIME SECURITY
Protect U.S. maritime borders by halting the flow of illegal drugs, migrants, and contraband, preventing illegal incursions into the U.S. exclusive economic zone, and suppressing violations of law in U.S. maritime regions.

NATIONAL DEFENSE
Defend the nation as one of the five armed services. Enhance regional stability in support of the National Security Strategy.

PROTECTION OF NATURAL RESOURCES
Stop environmental damage and natural resource degradation associated with maritime activities, commercial fishing, and recreational boating.

MARITIME SAFETY
Prevent deaths, injuries, and property damage associated with maritime transportation, offshore industry, fishing, and recreational boating.

MARITIME MOBILITY
Facilitate maritime commerce and eliminate interruptions and impediments to the economical movement of goods and people while maximizing recreational access to and enjoyment of the water.

The nation's cutters lack adequate speed, endurance, and systems to accomplish their missions in the most cost-effective manner. Aircraft and cutters have inferior sensors and limited night operations capability. Systems for communicating between Coast Guard units—as well as with the forces of other services or agencies and foreign coast guards—are inadequate. Antiquated technology increases the Coast Guard's operating and maintenance costs.

We can and must do better.

Curiously, the block obsolescence of many of the Coast Guard's most important assets is both a threat and an opportunity. It is a threat in that the service soon will be overwhelmed by a mismatch between its roles and missions and the quantity and quality of assets it has to carry them out. But it is an opportunity in that the Coast Guard is in a good position to take advantage of leading-edge technologies and systems, and the innovative operational concepts they enable, to meet its requirements more effectively and efficiently—if needed resources can be allocated.

Since 1998, the Coast Guard has been addressing these issues, and it has put in place the Deepwater Project, which will develop and field an integrated system of cutters, aircraft, and C^4ISR systems to meet the nation's maritime security needs. Instead of focusing on replacing specific hardware—like a class of cutter or aircraft—the Coast Guard has focused the Deepwater Project on the fundamental capabilities the service needs to perform all of its missions in the deepwater regions. In essence, the project is built on three pillars:

- A mission-based performance approach that describes fundamental mission requirements and focuses acquisition on mission accomplishment rather than on unique asset capabilities
- The need to maximize operational effectiveness while minimizing ownership costs
- Comprehensive modeling and simulation to develop a system that balances effectiveness with affordability

As part of the task force's assessment of the Deepwater Project, we concluded that the Coast Guard must have a "national security cutter" to fulfill its national defense missions. In addition, as a result of the national security requirements promulgated by the National Command Authority and regional commanders-in-chief, we recommended that future Coast Guard cutters and assets have the following national-defense-related characteristics:

- Speed, endurance, sea-keeping, and weapon systems to perform national defense missions effectively throughout the world in a variety of sea conditions

- Robust C^4ISR and defensive capabilities to be able to compel compliance for law enforcement and safely perform assigned national defense missions
- Capability to launch and recover aircraft as well as board and seize vessels in a variety of weather conditions
- Capability to surveil, detect, classify, identify, and prosecute targets of interest
- Interoperability with Navy assets, as well as with other regional assets

The Course Ahead

Throughout the 21st century, the United States will need efficient and reliable waterways. It will need a guardian of safety on the water and a protector of marine resources. It will need a front line of defense to protect our homeland against a host of threats and illicit activities that will come from the sea. And it will need a specialized naval force capable of operating alongside the other U.S. armed forces to support the nation's security strategies and policies at home and abroad. In short, the nation will need a world-class coast guard. If the U.S. Coast Guard did not exist, we would have to invent it, quickly.

The task force has voiced its overwhelming support for the Coast Guard, but the service cannot go it alone. It requires more support now from the administration and Congress to solve its current readiness shortfalls and to continue to pursue the recapitalization of its deepwater assets. Only after this support is received, and these initiatives are realized, will America's maritime guardian be "Always Ready" to meet the daunting threats and challenges that lay ahead.

Notes

1. The task force report is available on the Coast Guard's website at http://www.uscg.mil/news/rolesandmissions.html.
2. The Integrated Deepwater Capabilities Replacement Project (Deepwater Project) is the service's ongoing plan to recapitalize and modernize its fleet of cutters, aircraft, and afloat and ashore command, control, communications, computer, intelligence, surveillance, and reconnaissance assets. Deepwater missions are defined as those occurring beyond 50 nautical miles from U.S. shores.

9 "CONSTANCY AMID GREAT CHANGE"

ADM Thomas Collins, USCG

September 11 forever changed the U.S. Coast Guard. This August 2002 *Proceedings* article by Admiral Thomas Collins, twenty-second commandant of the U.S. Coast Guard, is important because it spells out the many changes that occurred in the U.S. Coast Guard in the immediate aftermath of September 11, 2001. The U.S. Coast Guard went from a peacetime setting to a wartime posture in a matter of hours to prevent a maritime terrorist attack, and it did so without neglecting any of its eleven missions and amid great organizational changes. The U.S. Coast Guard faced a daunting task to safeguard our 95,000 miles of waterways, 361 ports, 16,000-plus shipping containers entering the United States, cruise ships, foreign-flagged vessels, nuclear power plants, etc. Historians will look back at the numerous changes outlined by Admiral Collins to see how the U.S. Coast Guard made America's waterways safe from attack after 9/11.

"CONSTANCY AMID GREAT CHANGE"

By ADM Thomas Collins, USCG, U.S. Naval Institute *Proceedings* (August 2002): 32–37.

More than 225 years ago, as the fledgling American republic confronted its most serious national security challenge, Benjamin Franklin understood that "we must all hang together, or assuredly we shall all hang separately."

Today, the United States confronts its most serious national security challenge of the new century. The terrorist strikes of 11 September were the "shots heard 'round the world" in a war against global terrorism—a war we must win. In so doing, the Coast Guard must "hang together" with all other vital elements of the nation's homeland security and defense framework.

As President George W. Bush recognized when he proposed the creation of a new Department of Homeland Security, the Coast Guard is a unique instrument for safeguarding U.S. sovereignty, maritime safety and security, and defense. In our third century of operations, we must transform in select, key areas while holding fast to our core characteristics as a maritime, multimission, military service and continuing to embrace our core values of honor, respect, and devotion to duty.

Threats and Challenges to U.S. Maritime Safety and Security

Prior to 11 September, we recognized the increasing risk of transnational and unconventional threats. A 1999 Navy–Coast Guard intelligence assessment predicted a broad range of challenges to U.S. homeland security—migrant and drug smuggling; arms trafficking; proliferation of weapons of mass destruction and disruption; piracy and crimes at sea and in ports; terrorist attacks against ports and coastal population centers; overexploitation of maritime resources; environmental degradation; and more. Other studies and assessments—by the Office of Naval Intelligence, the Hart-Rudman Commission, and the Quadrennial Defense Reviews, to name a few—envisaged global and regional trends greatly increasing the need to protect U.S. maritime sovereignty and borders.

That said, the 11 September strikes proved that U.S. borders are dangerously porous, vital U.S. assets are surprisingly vulnerable, and our homeland is at grave risk from devastating attacks.

Countering maritime threats and challenges and ensuring the sanctity and efficiency of the U.S. marine transportation system (MTS) are principal responsibilities of the Coast Guard; however, we cannot do the job alone. Clearly we must cooperate closely with a number of departments and agencies at the national, regional, and local levels of government, as well as with private international organizations and other countries' governments and military services. This close collaboration with stakeholders and partners has been a Coast Guard strength for many years.

But we face considerable operational, material, and personnel challenges that are creating significant shortfalls in our overall capability and capacity. The service is hamstrung by a block obsolescence problem that has been exacerbated by chronic funding constraints. Our deepwater forces lack fundamental capabilities necessary for safe, efficient, and effective mission performance. Cutters have insufficient speed to prosecute contacts; in some cases, they can be outrun by drug-smugglers' go-fast boats. Cutters and aircraft have poor sensors and night operations capability, and there is limited interoperability between these platforms. Some medium-endurance cutters lack flight deck hangars and cannot deploy with helicopters, and the HH-60 medium-range helicopter is too large to land safely on all but a few cutters.

Inadequate communications and limited access to mission-critical information also create hurdles. Many cutters and aircraft can communicate only by voice, deployed cutters and aircraft often lack real-time or even near-real-time access to essential operational intelligence, and cutters and aircraft have limited ability to share tactical information and situational awareness. The Coast Guard's command, control, communications, computers, intelligence, surveillance, and reconnaissance (C^4ISR) infrastructure is increasingly incapable of meeting the full range of maritime domain awareness needs in critical operating areas.

As our assets continue to age, they place greater demands on the service's people and the logistics and support infrastructure. Spare parts shortages plague both fixed-wing aircraft and helicopters, the overall logistics effort demands more labor hours, and maintenance costs increase while cutter and aircraft operational availability decreases.

The good news is that on 25 June, the Coast Guard announced the award of the Integrated Deepwater Systems Program contract to the Integrated Coast Guard Systems (ICGS) team—a joint venture led by Lockheed Martin and Northrop Grumman. This multibillion-dollar program will include the acquisition of new Deepwater ships, fixed-wing aircraft, helicopters, and unmanned aerial vehicles; upgrade of existing cutters and helicopters; and development of C^4ISR and logistics systems. While a continuous, annual funding stream from Congress still is needed for the Deepwater Program to reach fruition, the contract award is a significant step toward achieving our future operational requirements.

Beyond Business as Usual

This situation has been made more complex by the reality of operations over the past 12 months, during which our roles, missions, and tasks have been all but turned upside down. Given resource and capacity restraints, enforcing fishery laws and intercepting drug runners and illegal immigrants must be balanced against the higher priority missions of port and coastal security. In addition to maintaining a strong search-and-rescue capability, the Coast Guard has refocused on the enormous task of protecting the United States' 361 ports and 95,000 miles of shoreline from all adversaries. More than 8,000 foreign-flag ships call at U.S. ports each year, carrying some 7 million containers, any one of which could be loaded with a weapon of mass destruction. Fewer than 3% of these are inspected, driving the need for the Coast Guard to "push out our borders" to interdict threats farther out to sea.

This "new normalcy," as my predecessor Admiral Jim Loy described it in late fall 2001, is a completely different ball game. In the immediate aftermath of

11 September, we threw everything at safeguarding our port and coastal areas, and while we have since pulled back some of those resources and reapplied them to more traditional responsibilities, it will never again be "business as usual" for the Coast Guard.

In all of this, we have been faced with "pay me now or pay me later" dilemmas. Last year, for example—before the homeland-security emergency prompted Congress to appropriate an additional $43 billion for U.S. security and defense needs—the Coast Guard was facing severely constrained funding, such that operations had to be cut by 10%, and then by another 25%, just to make ends meet. We were planning to retire or take assets out of service to help bridge the dollar gaps: three cutters, two ex-Navy ocean-surveillance ships and their eight deployable pursuit boats, three HH-65 Dolphin helicopters, three HC130s, and 13 HU-25 Falcon jets (half the force). Two air facilities—on Long Island, New York, and in Muskegon, Michigan—were planned for closure.

Since then, the Coast Guard has sought a balance among competing missions. Our operational profile clearly is different from a year ago, and our ability to anticipate and respond to new threats, risks, requirements, and opportunities is critical to our success. Reordered and expanded priorities have been met by a significant increase in supplemental funding for fiscal year 2002, and the Bush administration has proposed the largest funding increase in Coast Guard history—a 28% increase to $7.3 billion—for the new fiscal year that begins on 1 October.

Under our still-evolving mission set, our maritime homeland security mission would represent approximately 27% of the Coast Guard budget. Search-and-rescue funding would remain stable at 12%, but it would be an increase in actual dollars compared to previous years. Fisheries enforcement and drug interdiction both would see a decline in budget share—from 16% to 11% and from 18% to 13%, respectively—but looking at percentages is misleading because the overall budget is increasing. Fisheries enforcement operations, for instance, would receive $504 million, up from $440 million.

Overall, the budget request is adequate for the Coast Guard to cover maritime safety and security duties and start making critical improvements, such as buying new cutters and aircraft for deepwater missions, increasing personnel at understaffed small-boat stations, and buying a new maritime command, control, and response system. We are putting in place a refocused maritime strategy and comprehensive program for out-year funding that is both sufficient and stable to help guarantee that all of our missions can be accomplished. If we are able to sustain a multiyear resource ramp-up along the lines of fiscal year 2003, we will be in a good position to address existing capability and capacity gaps.

Refining Our Strategic Vision

The Coast Guard has been at the center of a multiagency effort to define a maritime security strategy to complement the broader homeland security strategy. There are five principal elements of the maritime homeland security strategy: (1) ensuring maritime domain awareness; (2) monitoring and controlling the movement of high-interest vessels; (3) enhancing our presence and response capabilities in domestic ports and harbors, in our territorial sea, and on the high seas; (4) protecting critical infrastructure; and (5) increasing domestic and international outreach.

Prior to 11 September, our awareness of potential maritime threats to the United States was relatively low. Our preparations were focused primarily on a first-response capability and then consequence management and remediation. If we hope to prevent future catastrophic events such as the terrorist attacks against New York and Washington, we must have significantly more knowledge of our vulnerabilities and the threats against us. Guaranteeing maritime domain awareness, therefore, is our primary strategic concern.

Most fundamentally, maritime domain awareness means we possess a comprehensive knowledge of our vulnerabilities, threats, and targets of interest on the water. It requires more aggressive and more effective means of gathering, using, and sharing information and intelligence in the maritime and naval domain than has ever been possible in the past. There are other important attributes, as well:

- Knowledge that grows increasingly comprehensive and specific as activities and potential threats move closer to the United States; for vast oceanic regions, the knowledge can be less specific
- Extensive knowledge of geography, weather, position of friendly and unfriendly forces, trends, key indicators, anomalies, intent, and the activities of all vessels within an area of concern
- New data-mining and reach-back techniques and databases shared across traditional agency and department boundaries
- Intelligence fusion centers to collect, fuse, and analyze all-source intelligence—an important element that figured into the proposal for a Homeland Security Department
- A single integrated operating picture for afloat and ashore operating forces of relevant, timely, accurate, scalable, and reliable information within an area of interest

Above all, maritime domain awareness has to do with having access to detailed data and comprehensive knowledge about our adversaries and ourselves, sharing that information more effectively among federal agencies and with our domestic and international partners in both the private and public sectors, and being able to act on it in real time.

Second, to ensure we can control the movement of any vessel that could be used as a weapon of mass destruction, we must detect, identify, monitor, board, and inspect what we characterize as high-interest vessels. The Coast Guard now screens all foreign-flag vessels greater than 300 gross tons, requiring them to provide a 96-hour advance notice of arrival. Security checks are conducted on the information provided by these vessels, including crew lists and passengers on board. We also board at sea, well before they enter port, certain other high-interest vessels—ships that might have called at ports in countries known to support terrorist groups, for example—and escort others into port to reduce potential for hijacking.

In our fiscal year 2003 budget request, we have asked for 160 sea marshals for armed escort of these vessels, as well as resources to increase on-the-water patrols for all 49 captains of the port. These sea marshals also will provide surge capability to maritime regions in the event of increased threat levels.

Third, to enhance presence and response capabilities, we need to detect, intercept, and interdict potential threats as far out to sea as possible, to defeat criminal or catastrophic events well before they threaten our shores. To do so, we are developing a layered defense capability.

We will employ boats, cutters, and aircraft to increase presence wherever the United States has key interests. Coast Guard counterdrug and migrant interdiction efforts strike at funding sources for organized crime and terrorism, and our migrant interdiction patrols deter foreign terrorists from crossing our borders.

We will continue to partner closely with the Navy. The Coast Guard and the Navy have refined, updated, and expanded the 1998 National Fleet Policy statement to improve interoperability of our ships and aircraft and coordination between our services, including the sharing of important assets. For example, 13 Navy *Cyclone* (PC-1)–class patrol boats are under Coast Guard command to protect vital coastal areas. We, in turn, can provide highly capable port security units to assist in the waterside security of Navy assets both at home and abroad.

Additional presence in our ports and coastal waters will come from six new Coast Guard maritime safety and security teams (MSSTs), comprised of nearly 420 active-duty and 180 reserve personnel, as well as 70 additional port security response boats and increased staffing for small-boat stations. Funding for these new units has been requested in our fiscal year 2003 budget. Ultimately, we plan to expand up to 12 MSSTs for rapid-response surge operations from key home ports throughout the United States. We think of these MSSTs as domestic counterparts to our expeditionary port security units.

Fourth, we have identified and established interim measures to protect critical infrastructures in all 49 captain of the port zones. These infrastructures include everything from national icons, such as the Statue of Liberty, to critical nuclear power plants. For fiscal year 2003, we have requested $51 million for antiterrorism and force protection, requiring specific enhancements to physical infrastructure, cybersecurity, personal protective equipment, chemical weapons of mass destruction detection equipment, and weapons.

Fifth, to increase domestic and international outreach, the Coast Guard will strengthen partnerships and strategic relationships at home and abroad. We need effective security plans for commercial vessels, offshore structures, and waterfront facilities, but because so many of the critical facilities and vessels of concern are owned and operated by the private sector, and because of the need to be fiscally responsible, the Coast Guard cannot, and should not, do it all. We have to work this problem collaboratively with our federal partners, including the Federal Bureau of Investigation, Central Intelligence Agency, Immigration and Naturalization Service, Border Patrol, and Transportation Security Administration; with state and local authorities; with key private marine stakeholders; and internationally. On the international scene, we have been working with the International Maritime Organization (IMO) to improve security on vessels that may call at U.S. ports.

Another important aspect of our maritime homeland security vision, and one that ultimately could determine our success or failure, is our ability to detect, deter, disrupt, and interdict all threats as far from our homeland as possible. The emerging maritime security strategy calls for multiagency, multinational, layered operations that push our maritime borders out to sea—well beyond our 200-mile exclusive economic zone. As a result of our counter-narcotics operations and illegal migrant patrols, the Coast Guard has realized for some time that the U.S. "frontier" begins where the threat originates—at the country of origin.

To safeguard the U.S. homeland, we must be active far from our own coasts. For example, because it is impossible to inspect every ship calling at our seaports or in transit in U.S. territorial waters, we instead use risk-based decision making, based on extensive knowledge of our vulnerabilities and threats, to employ a broad array of safety and security regimes. Working with the IMO and foreign governments, we will seek to identify cargoes loaded in foreign ports and destined for the United States, to maintain good in-transit monitoring and to avoid a maritime-security shell game.

Three Key Management Focus Areas

My most important emphasis is our commitment to our people. Our people make the Coast Guard what it is. They ensure our operational excellence. Coast Guard personnel will operate in an increasingly more complex and technologically sophisticated environment, characterized by new Deepwater cutters, superior response boats, upgraded aircraft systems, advanced command, control, and communication systems, and greater information connectivity at all levels of the organization. Transforming the service with this new technology requires that we transform our dedicated and professional workforce with the same care and foresight.

The ability to attract, develop, retain, and deploy a quality workforce is key to the Coast Guard's success. This is my top priority and, perhaps, our greatest challenge. It will mean restructuring decades-old human-resource policies and processes, ensuring compensation parity with the Department of Defense, building an innovative training and professional development program, and appealing to a diverse pool of candidates. Accordingly, we will:

- Emphasize education, training, and professional growth for all elements of the workforce
- Grow the workforce to meet increasing mission demands
- Identify new strategies to recruit, train, deploy, and retain a diverse, highly capable, and flexible workforce
- Implement restructured personnel, operations, and support systems that guide assignment and advancement
- Factor human-factors engineering and human-systems integration into the design, engineering, and acquisition of new hardware and information-technology systems, as well as into the implementation of new policies driven by the changing security environment

Our goal is to attain greater stability and flexibility for the workforce and achieve better quality of service—which includes both quality of life and quality of work and workplace.

Readiness means the Coast Guard will be capable, competent, and vigilant in all mission areas. Superior operational service is our core purpose, and we have long been recognized as the world's best coast guard. The nation expects that we will bring the same level of professionalism and maritime leadership to the war on terrorism as has been reflected in the conduct of all our missions. Although homeland security is a pressing concern, the Coast Guard's other missions of ensuring maritime security, maritime safety, protection of natural resources, maritime mobility, and national defense have not waned. In short, we must be ready in all of our mission areas, while building our maritime security capability as a priority.

As the lead federal agency for maritime safety and maritime homeland security, we will ensure that our units employ sound and safe doctrine and tactics; are supported with responsive, integrated logistics systems; are adequately staffed with trained and motivated people; and are equipped with modern and well-maintained cutters, boats, aircraft, equipment, and facilities. Units will operate to the level that our support systems can sustain, within prescribed employment and crew fatigue standards, while aggressively managing risk. To improve our current and future readiness we will:

- Build strong maritime homeland security strategies, capabilities, and competencies
- Design and implement a maritime domain awareness capability that provides integrated afloat, ashore, and airborne C^4ISR focused on meeting both the informational needs of decision makers and the tactical needs of operational commanders
- Ensure supporting command, control, and communications organizational structures exist at the port level to meet tactical mission objectives
- Ensure our future readiness by leveraging the Integrated Deepwater System Program, the National Distress and Response System Modernization Project, and near-term homeland security initiatives as significant steps in the strategic recapitalization of our operational and support capability

- Build strategic partnerships to enhance mission outcomes at all levels—federal, state, and local; international, regional, and bilateral; public and private—to bring clarity to mission planning and execution and to leverage the capabilities of Coast Guard forces and force structure

My final area of emphasis is stewardship. We will work hard to strengthen our reputation for excellence in managing our resources by installing quality principles in all we do, by emphasizing performance-based planning and resource allocation, and by driving to a culture of innovation and smart use of technology. We will be accountable for delivering results. Good stewardship means that the Coast Guard is aligned from top to bottom and bottom to top, and that we embrace innovation, technology, and effective management practices to achieve measurable outcomes.

Knowing who we are, what we do, how we do it, and why we do it is critical. Engaging our strengths and capabilities, and unleashing our collective ingenuity and resourcefulness as we consider how to accomplish every mission, is imperative. We must continue and expand our commitment to customer-focused and outcome-based operations. We must exhort our people to identify and embrace necessary change, employ their creative talents, share new ideas, and deliver the highest quality service to the American public. To strengthen our stewardship of the public trust we will:

- Strive to be the best-led and best-managed organization in the federal government
- Inspire a culture of innovation and process change, and ensure the creative infusion of technology in all mission areas to enhance productivity and reduce workload, while driving toward quality outcomes
- Take advantage of the opportunities presented by our systems acquisition initiatives—exemplified by our Integrated Deepwater System Program—through which we will develop strategic relationships with vendors and revolutionize our operational and support processes to the advantage of the U.S. taxpayer, Coast Guard people, and overall service excellence

- Deliver measurable results that support the President's management agenda, and directly contribute to achieving the desired outcomes of the Department of Transportation and Coast Guard strategic plans

The Course Ahead

During many crises and virtually every conflict since 1790, the United States has entrusted the Coast Guard with critical missions—many that no other agency could or would perform. Each time, we accepted the challenge and folded it into our inventory of multimission responsibilities. Nearly 100 years ago, for example, the *Titanic* tragedy was a key catalyst in the transformation of the Revenue Cutter Service and related maritime safety and security agencies into the modern U.S. Coast Guard. So, too, the events of 11 September look to argue for a Coast Guard renaissance for the 21st century. If, indeed, Congress approves the President's request to establish a new Department of Homeland Security, the Coast Guard will adjust to that change and be ready to do what is necessary to ensure that maritime homeland safety and security are guaranteed.

The new century promises increasing demand for the services the Coast Guard provides. The nation's interconnection to the rest of the world will magnify the importance of an efficient and safe marine transportation system, of security from terrorist attack and criminal enterprises, of protection of living marine resources and the marine environment, and of the continued preservation of our liberty and prosperity. The maritime dimensions of the threats that will challenge our citizens, interests, and friends are real, growing, and clearly "Coast Guard business." So it is that the Coast Guard, the smallest of the five U.S. military services, has a broad and ever-increasing mandate for ensuring maritime safety and security and sustaining its national and international leadership in all of its mission areas.

As we respond to this call for action, we must place our immediate action on strengthening our maritime security capabilities, with a watchful eye on our entire mission set and the need to "hang together" with all other actors that contribute to the nation's security. By improving our ability to provide maritime security to the United States, we will improve our capability in all our mission areas. Every Coast Guard mission is connected [to the other missions], and excellence in all is the rightful expectation of all U.S. citizens. Most fundamentally, however, we must be forever vigilant and always ready to answer the call.

PART II

U.S. Coast Guard Missions

10 "MISSIONS"

(Selection from chapter 2 of *The Coast Guardsman's Manual, 11th Edition*)

Jim Dolbow

There is a common saying in the Coast Guard that every day is like game day. The U.S. Coast Guard has eleven statutory missions. They are all detailed in chapter 2 of *The Coast Guardsman's Manual, 11th Edition*. To understand the U.S. Coast Guard, you need to understand its missions.

"MISSIONS"

(Selection from chapter 2 of *The Coast Guardsman's Manual, 11th Edition*) by Jim Dolbow (Naval Institute Press, 2017): 25–29.

By law the Coast Guard has eleven statutory missions that are defined as either "homeland security" or "non-homeland security." These missions clearly demonstrate how the Coast Guard's assets, competencies, capabilities, authorities, and partnerships bring forth a unique ability to serve as a leading maritime responder and incident manager within government.

Homeland Security Missions

Defense Readiness

As one of the nation's five armed services, the Coast Guard provides unique authorities and capabilities to support our nation's war plans. These unique authorities and capabilities provided under the Defense Operations program encompass eight activities: maritime interdiction operations, combating maritime terrorism, port operations security and defense, military environmental response operations, coastal sea control operations, maritime operational threat response, rotary wing air intercept operations, and support for theater security cooperation initiatives. They are essential military tasks assigned to the Coast Guard as a component of joint and combined forces in peacetime, crisis, and war.

Moreover, outside of U.S. coastal waters, the Coast Guard assists foreign naval and maritime forces through training and joint operations. Many of the world's maritime nations have forces that operate principally in the littoral seas and conduct missions that resemble those of the U.S. Coast Guard and not the U.S. Navy. Since it has such a varied mix of assets and missions, the Coast Guard is a powerful role model that is in ever-increasing demand abroad. The service's close working relations with these nations not only improve mutual cooperation during specific joint operations in which the Coast Guard is involved but also support U.S. diplomatic efforts in general: the promotion of democracy, economic prosperity, and trust between nations.

Ports, Waterways, and Coastal Security (PWCS)

The PWCS mission entails the protection of the U.S. maritime domain and the U.S. Marine Transportation System (MTS) and those who live, work, or recreate near them; the prevention and disruption of terrorist attacks, sabotage, espionage, or subversive acts; and the response to and recovery from those acts that do occur. Conducting PWCS deters terrorists from using or exploiting the MTS as a means for attacks on U.S. territory, population centers, vessels, critical infrastructure, and key resources. PWCS includes employing awareness activities; conducting counterterrorism, antiterrorism, preparedness, and response operations; and establishing and overseeing a maritime security regime. PWCS also includes the national defense role of protecting military outload operations.

Drug Interdiction

The Coast Guard is the lead federal agency for maritime drug interdiction and shares lead responsibility for air interdiction with the U.S. Customs Service. As such, it is a key player in combating the flow of illegal drugs to the United States. The Coast Guard's mission is to reduce the supply of drugs from the source by denying smugglers the use of air and maritime routes in the transit zone, a 6-million-square-mile area that includes the Caribbean, Gulf of Mexico, and Eastern Pacific. In meeting the challenge of patrolling this vast area, the Coast Guard coordinates closely with other federal agencies and countries within the region to disrupt and deter the flow of illegal drugs.

Migrant Interdiction

The Coast Guard is the lead agency for the enforcement of U.S. immigration laws at sea. It conducts patrols and coordinates with other federal agencies and foreign countries to interdict undocumented migrants at sea, denying them entry via maritime routes to the United States, its territories, and possessions. Thousands of people try to enter this country illegally every year using maritime routes, many via smuggling operations. Interdicting migrants at sea means they can be quickly returned to their countries of origin without the costly processes required if they were to successfully enter the United States. Coast Guard migrant-interdiction operations in the Caribbean, the Gulf of Mexico, and the Eastern Pacific are as much humanitarian efforts as they are law enforcement missions. In fact, the majority of migrant-interdiction cases handled by the Coast Guard actually begin as search-and-rescue missions, usually on the high seas rather than in U.S. coastal waters.

Other Law Enforcement

Preventing illegal foreign fishing vessel encroachment in the exclusive economic zone is a primary Coast Guard role vital to protecting the integrity of the nation's maritime borders and ensuring the health of U.S. fisheries. The Coast Guard also enforces international agreements to suppress damaging illegal, unreported, and unregulated fishing activity on the high seas.

Non-Homeland Security Missions

Marine Safety

The Marine Safety program ensures the safe operation and navigation of U.S.- and foreign-flagged vessels. The Coast Guard is responsible for providing safe, efficient, and environmentally sound waterways for commercial and recreational users. Domestic vessel inspections and port state control (foreign vessel) examinations are conducted in order to safeguard maritime commerce and international trade.

Search and Rescue

Search and rescue (SAR) is one of the Coast Guard's oldest missions and perhaps the Coast Guard's best-known mission area. Minimizing the loss of life, injury, and property damage by rendering aid to persons in distress and property at risk in the maritime environment has always been a Coast Guard priority. Coast Guard SAR response involves multimission stations, cutters, aircraft, and boats linked by communications networks.

The National SAR Plan divides the U.S. area of SAR responsibility into internationally recognized inland and maritime SAR regions. The Coast Guard is the maritime SAR coordinator. To meet this responsibility, the Coast Guard maintains SAR facilities on the East, West, and Gulf coasts, in Alaska, Hawaii, Guam, and Puerto Rico, and on the Great Lakes and inland U.S. waterways. When the rescue alarm sounds, the Coast Guard is ready to confront the inherently dangerous maritime environment, frequently going into harm's way to save others. The Coast Guard works closely with other federal, state, and local agencies, and with foreign nations, to provide the world's fastest and most effective response to distress calls. It also maintains a vessel-tracking system called AMVER (automated mutual assistance vessel rescue) that allows it to divert nearby commercial vessels to render assistance when necessary.

Aids to Navigation

The aids-to-navigation mission is a means for the Coast Guard to mark the waters of the United States and its territories to assist boaters in navigation and alert them to obstructions and hazards.

Living Marine Resources

The Living Marine Resources program's mission is to provide effective and professional at-sea enforcement of federal fisheries regulations and other regulations to advance national goals for the conservation and management of living marine resources and their environments through the detection and deterrence of illegal fishing activity. Beginning with the protection of the Bering Sea fur seal and sea otter herds and continuing through the vast expansion following World War II in the size and efficiency of global fishing fleets, Coast Guard responsibilities in this mission area now include enforcement of laws and treaties in the 3.36-million-square-mile U.S. exclusive economic zone, the largest in the world.

Marine Environmental Protection

The Marine Environmental Protection program falls under the Coast Guard's stewardship role. It is concerned with averting the introduction of invasive species, stopping unauthorized ocean dumping, and preventing the discharge of oil or hazardous substances into the navigable waters of the United States.

Ice Operations

The ice operations mission encompasses icebreaking activities in the Great Lakes, Saint Lawrence Seaway, and Northeast. These activities facilitate the movement of bulk cargoes carried by regional commercial fleets during the winter months. In addition to domestic ice operations, the Coast Guard operates the only U.S.-controlled icebreakers capable of operations in the polar regions.

Coast Guard Intelligence

While intelligence collection is not a statutory mission of the Coast Guard, it is vital to the conduct of the Coast Guard's missions. The Coast Guard is singular among seventeen agencies that make up the Intelligence Community (IC) for its national and law enforcement intelligence statutory authorities in the maritime domain. Thus, the Coast Guard is uniquely positioned to provide actionable, timely, and fused intelligence to its operational commanders and IC partners.

11 "THE COAST GUARD'S TRIDENT"

CDR Bruce B. Stubbs, USCG

Bruce Stubbs is one of the Coast Guard's best minds. This was evident in this June 1986 *Proceedings* article entitled "The Coast Guard's Trident." Stubbs' writings have appeared throughout *Proceedings* over the years, highlighting the importance of the Coast Guard's national defense mission. Arguably, the national defense mission is the Coast Guard's most important mission because without it, all the other missions are moot. Unfortunately, as Stubbs points out in this article, the Coast Guard's national defense mission was underfunded in comparison to some of the Coast Guard's other non-homeland security missions. Written in 1986 when the author was a commander assigned to President Ronald Reagan's National Security Council staff, "The Coast Guard's Trident" is a timeless article.

"THE COAST GUARD'S TRIDENT"

By CDR Bruce B. Stubbs, USCG, U.S. Naval Institute *Proceedings* (June 1986): 50–55.

As Commandant of the Coast Guard for the past four years, Admiral James S. Gracey has testified before Congress that the Coast Guard's three basic missions—defense readiness, maritime safety, and maritime law enforcement—have equal priority. However, not all Coast Guardsmen agree with this view. Some consider defense readiness as being outside the mainstream of Coast Guard activities and undeserving of equal emphasis.

Most Coast Guard personnel work in maritime safety and maritime law enforcement assignments, and their responsibilities do not routinely expose them to defense requirements or issues. Some do not foresee circumstances requiring the mobilization or the combat employment of the Coast Guard. As members of an operationally oriented agency, they share the reluctance of many personnel of these "now" organizations—they do not like to get involved with what they perceive as a "paper" program.

Further compounding this skewed assessment is a lack of internal consensus on the Coast Guard's fundamental reason for existence. If there were no need for a federal maritime safety and law enforcement agency, and if there were no need for performing these missions, there would be no requirement for the Coast Guard. The service's defense readiness mission is a result of its existence and is not the Coast Guard's *raison d'être*. However, by federal statutes the Coast Guard is an armed force and is required to be ready to serve as a specialized service in the U.S. Navy.

To assume that the Coast Guard will remain uninvolved in a crisis belies its record of wartime employment, belittles previous contributions, and ignores present-day resource and threat realities. Coast Guardsmen must not assume the next war will either be nuclear or over before the Coast Guard can get into action. From the fall of the Shah of Iran to the Falklands Conflict, professional analysts have failed to predict events. Likewise, Coast Guardsmen cannot safely speculate that their service will have no role in a conflict or a peacetime contingency.

In a conventional conflict, Commanders-in-Chief Atlantic and Pacific (CinCLant/CinCPac) would use available resources. If the lessons of history are correct, commanders-in-chief have always lacked sufficient ships, aircraft, and personnel to accomplish their mission. Admiral Wesley L. McDonald, then-CinCLant, stated in an *Armed Forces Journal* interview just last year:

"I am approximately 50% short in escorts and I won't be able to provide escorts for all my convoys going across the Atlantic." He also said that he was short aircraft and mine warfare assets.

Coast Guard resources not only help reduce this shortfall, but also release Navy assets to forward deploy to high-threat areas. In addition, other Coast Guard forces are slated to protect U.S. and foreign ports, to oversee fuel and ammunition handling, and a host of other theater support activities. And, most important, the Navy can depend on the Coast Guard to be present for duty when called.

An aggressive Soviet foreign policy, Third World events, and the Navy's global involvement and platform shortages have stretched the Navy's forces to their limits. The commanders-in-chief cannot ignore the ready availability of Coast Guard resources, especially in today's declining defense budget environment. The Coast Guard is a naval augmentation force-in-being. Providing more than 189 aircraft, more than 240 cutters (65 feet or longer), and approximately 39,000 active-duty and 12,500 reserve personnel, the Coast Guard can act as a force multiplier for the commanders-in-chief.

Because the Coast Guard is an armed force of the United States with valuable resources and trained military personnel, the service can be usefully employed. The defense readiness mission is a basic Coast Guard mission and must be accepted as such.

How can a better view of the defense readiness mission be developed among all Coast Guard professionals? A greater familiarity with events in the lesser developed countries, the Soviet threat, the Navy's responsibilities, and the many operating plans requiring Coast Guard participation would make the service's defense readiness role more evident to all Coast Guardsmen.

The Coast Guard must be equipped and trained for predetermined wartime missions jointly approved by the Coast Guard and the Navy. To conduct these wartime missions, the Coast Guard must do advanced planning and commit some of its resources to ready the service for wartime or contingency use. Effective wartime mission execution strongly suggests that Coast Guard peacetime activities closely parallel its wartime activities, and that scarce Coast

Guard funds not be used to duplicate equipment and services already existing in the other armed forces. This does not mean the Coast Guard should become a mini-Navy, only that it should prepare to conduct its wartime tasking effectively. When it is feasible, interoperability and commonality of its equipment and procedures with those of the other armed services should be a national requirement.

Recognition of this requirement is not new. In an 1885 *Proceedings* article, Navy Ensign W. I. Chambers suggested that the Navy control the design of the Revenue Marine cutters to ensure these ships could serve as combatants. About the same time, the first director of the Office of Naval Intelligence wrote in *Proceedings* that the Revenue Marine and the Coast Survey vessels should provide coastal defense during wartime. He also wrote that the Lighthouse Establishment tenders should be used for harbor and coastal mining.

A century ago, these farsighted naval officers recognized the practicality of these organizations functioning effectively with the Navy. They knew that these forerunners of the Coast Guard would not be able to go their own way during a conflict and that the Navy would call upon them to contribute to a war effort. They also knew it made good economic sense to equip and train standing maritime forces. More than 100 years later, their observations remain valid. Although the Navy still does not design Coast Guard cutters, it does provide support to prepare the Coast Guard for wartime service.

In addition to the traditional Navy-supported program for cutter weapon systems, communications, and sensor equipment, the Navy and the Coast Guard have done much to strengthen their ties to one another. Prime examples are the establishment of the Navy/Coast Guard Board (NavGard) and the Office of Readiness and Reserve at Coast Guard Headquarters, the increased number of Coast Guard liaison officers working with the Navy, the increased participation of Coast Guard cutters and aircraft in Navy exercises, the extensive Navy participation in the *Hamilton* (WHEC-715)–class high-endurance cutters' fleet rehabilitation and modernizations (FRAMs), and the establishment of the Maritime Defense Zone commands. In addition, almost all Coast Guard flag officers have attended a tactical warfare planning course.

In the spring of 1985, the Office of Command, Control, and Communications (G-T) established with the Chief of Naval Operations (OpNav-904) a joint working group to coordinate Navy/Coast Guard command, control, and communications (C^3) requirements. Although it was established in 1981, G-T had no formal policy coordination procedures linking it with the Navy until the agreement in 1985. Some Coast Guard units may not be able to communicate with Navy units today, but this joint group will develop a plan to prevent system duplication and to ensure system compatibility between the Coast Guard and the Navy.

In the area of aircraft procurement, the Coast Guard is assessing the suitability of a variety of current or anticipated Navy helicopter procurements to satisfy its upcoming replacement of the HH-3F helicopter for the medium-range recovery mission requirement. By purchasing a DoD-common airframe, the Coast Guard would buy into the DoD-integrated logistics system and training infrastructure. This arrangement permits economies of scale and precludes duplication of system support at the wholesale level. The costs of logistics support for the foreign-made HU-25A Guardian and HH-65A Dolphin demonstrate the problems of operating non-DoD-supported airframes. The Navy would benefit by having additional compatible airframes, aircrews, and support personnel to draw upon in wartime by simply installing sensor avionics and weapon systems. The cost savings of this approach to the Coast Guard alone could be considerable. In contrast, by going its own way, the Coast Guard's hardware procurement support costs could skyrocket.

During wartime, the Guardian and Dolphin aircraft may not be supportable under the aegis of the Industrial Preparedness Program. Because they are foreign designs, there are few manufacturing companies in the United States to support these airframes. In addition, the HH-65A Dolphin helicopter engine is made by the same company that produces the engine used in the U.S. Army's M-1 main battle tank. Helicopter engine support during mobilization could be adversely affected by the Army's requirements.

Surface vessel logistics is the proverbial Achilles' heel of Coast Guard defense and operational readiness. Most Coast Guard equipment lacks allowance part list numbers, and many repair parts have no national stock numbers in addition to almost no centralized configuration management. Organizationally, the multiple responsibility for logistics by the Office of Command, Control, and Communications, Office of the Comptroller (G-F), and the Office of Engineering (G-E), rather than by one support manager, further handicaps the Coast Guard's logistics system. The logistics system that generated the need for an integrated logistics overhaul on the *Hamilton*s during their FRAMs is the same logistics system these cutters will return to after their modernizations.

The Coast Guard can neither achieve interoperability within the Navy nor conduct distant and remote operations if it cannot tell the Navy its logistical requirements. The 1980 Cuban Boat Lift, the 1981 Haitian Migrant Interdiction Operation start-up, the 1983 Grenada Operation (Urgent Fury), and the extensive 1984 drug interdiction operation (Wagon Wheel) demonstrated the need for a more effective logistics system to increase cutter operational availability. All in-house measures to improve the service's logistics posture must include input from the naval material establishment.

In order to achieve commonality and interoperability, the Navy must also realize that the Coast Guard has some unique needs that require support. For instance, the Coast Guard requirement for a law enforcement vessel intelligence sighting report could not be supported by the Navy's Rainform series of messages. The Coast Guard has developed its own sighting report entitled Summary Enforcement Event Report (SEER), to provide Coast Guard operational commands with vessel sighting data. Unlike the Rainform message series, however, SEER cannot be data-linked to a DoD command because it lacks DoD interface capability. Coast Guard cutters will use SEER on Coast Guard missions and shift to Rainform messages when they are under Navy orders. This lack of interoperability should be corrected. The joint C^3 picture is confused enough without additional complications, as the post-action report on the Grenada rescue operation so painfully demonstrated.

Even though the Coast Guard has substantially improved its coordination with the Navy, much remains to be done. However, improvements in commonality and interoperability with the Navy cannot be achieved solely by organizational procedures and liaison officers. A better understanding of the requirements of the Coast Guard's defense readiness mission is necessary.

The Coast Guard must develop a doctrine defining its relationship with the Navy and its role in wartime. There is no official policy statement outlining the goals and objectives of the Navy/Coast Guard relationship. Improved interoperability and commonality with the Navy will not be achieved until Coast Guard resource managers recognize the need for them. There is no justification for these needs, and the resource managers do not fully solicit the Navy's cooperation and input. A doctrine would provide the framework that planners, designers, and platform decision-makers require when making resource allocation decisions, and explain why program functions must be conducted with a view toward defense readiness implications. In addition, this doctrine would provide the basis for all Coast Guardsmen to understand why defense readiness is a shared responsibility regardless of one's individual assignment.

The Coast Guard must demonstrate that readiness billets are career enhancing, and not "career-killing backwater" assignments as was written by Coast Guard Lieutenant Commander Daniel W. Wood in his March 1985 comment in the *Proceedings* forum. Readiness billets rarely attract Coast Guard volunteers. Instead, they prefer duty in an active operational mission or a visible support area. Some Coast Guard officers see other assignments as more attractive, important, and rewarding, since they tend to view readiness assignments as out of the mainstream of Coast Guard activities. If all officers were armed with the knowledge that readiness tours are not career damaging, but rather are stepping stones to more responsible positions, more would actively seek readiness assignments.

The Coast Guard should task the NavGard Board with evaluating Coast Guard/Navy interoperability and commonality. This evaluation would serve as the plan of action for improvements in coordination and compatibility between the two naval services. The Navy, through its NavGard role, should play a greater role in the Coast Guard's platform selection process to coordinate interservice compatibility. This would facilitate the Coast Guard in conducting deliberate planning at the forefront of its resource acquisition process to address cost tradeoffs of building in defense capabilities.

The Coast Guard must encourage its senior officers to write more articles for professional journals. This would stimulate discussion of these important issues and would serve as an example to others that they, too, should be more aware and involved with these issues. *Proceedings* rarely publishes articles by Coast Guard senior leaders. Knowing that *Proceedings* is a forum for all the sea services and that our senior leaders can express themselves well, I can only assume that Coast Guard professionals are not writing. To stimulate more activity in this area, perhaps the Coast Guard Trust Fund could work with the U.S. Naval Institute to sponsor an annual essay contest with a $1,500 prize for the best essay on the Coast Guard's roles and missions; the winner would be published in *Proceedings*. Such an inducement should generate many articles and negate tasking all Coast Guard war college students to submit Coast Guard articles to professional journals.

To increase interservice understanding further, the Coast Guard should arrange to have a Navy officer and a Marine Corps officer assigned to the Coast Guard Academy—one as a company officer and the other to instruct a general naval science (sea power) course. A Coast Guard officer should be assigned to the Naval Academy. Both services would benefit by exposing their future entry-level officers to the other service. A Coast Guard senior officer should routinely be assigned to the Strategic Studies Group at the Naval War College. In addition, Coast Guard leadership should conduct an opinion poll of the officer corps to survey officers' attitudes toward defense readiness and other issues, similar to the recent U.S. Army poll on the officer corps' perception of general officer leadership. By reviewing the results of such a poll, Coast Guard leaders could determine if further corrective measures are required.

Another suggestion is to establish a mid-level management school, or Coast Guard Staff College (CGSC). This would provide the service with an ideal forum for developing an understanding of the service's defense readiness mission. Possibly, the existing Coast Guard Leadership and Management School's (LMS) resources could be converted into a CGSC, and the Navy's Leadership and Management and Effectiveness Training schools could be used to provide training for those who would have attended LMS, thus increasing the professional contact between the two services. The new staff school's primary function would be to develop and improve the following qualities within the officer corps:

- The ability to analyze and solve operational problems
- Effective communications skills
- The ability to interact and coordinate as a member of a staff
- An understanding of Coast Guard organization, operations, and procedures

Geared for lieutenants and lieutenant commanders, this school would be no longer than four weeks' duration. The curriculum might focus on such subjects as the Coast Guard planning and budget process, Coast Guard mission areas, and the Coast Guard's role in the federal government and national defense. This school would become the crossroads for Coast Guard professionals, producing officers well versed in the Coast Guard's history and concept as a multi-mission armed force, and familiar with the Coast Guard as a whole, its programs, its functions, and its philosophy as an agency.

These suggestions should increase contacts and understanding between the Coast Guard and the Navy, and should increase appreciation for the potential value of the Coast Guard's contribution to the Navy in a crisis. The Coast Guard is a defense bargain, and the Navy is being prudent when it trains and equips already existing Coast Guard resources in order to maximize the purchasing power of the nation's budget dollar. From fiscal year 1986 to fiscal year 1991, the Navy will fund $645 million worth of combat systems for Coast Guard platforms. More than half of this money will be used on the FRAMs for the 378-foot *Hamilton*-class cutters with impressive results. For approximately the cost of one *Oliver Hazard Perry* (FFG-7)–class frigate, the Navy and the nation gain 12 modern antisubmarine warfare (ASW) general-purpose frigate-type cutters.

The Coast Guard has more defense assets to offer. With a relatively small investment, these assets could make a substantial contribution if needed. The Coast Guard has 29 small, frigate-type cutters available for service with the Navy. The 16 210-foot medium-endurance cutters have an obsolete surface weapon, one surface search sensor, and a non-Navy certified flight deck, but no ASW capability. The 13 270-foot medium-endurance cutters have a Mk-92 fire control system with a Mk-75 gun mount, an SLQ-32 suite, and a flight deck; however, they also have no ASW capability. Naval warfare primary mission areas are not assigned to Coast Guard aircraft. Consequently, most of these valuable aircraft and their outstanding aircrews have no formal wartime tasking.

The measures suggested here should also facilitate a better appreciation of the defense readiness mission within the Coast Guard. The Coast Guard's difficulty in working out its dual-role character as a maritime safety and law enforcement agency operating in a civilian environment and a naval augmentation force-in-being awaiting the next conflict has hindered its planning for defense missions. It is only prudent for the Coast Guard to have effective mechanisms to coordinate with the Navy. Without them, nothing will prevent the consequences of their absence in conflict.

Coast Guard professionals must realize that they have three important and equal missions—maritime safety, defense readiness, and maritime law enforcement. The Coast Guardsman's role was best summarized by Rear Admiral F. C. Billard, the sixth Commandant of the Coast Guard, when he said: "Having fought as a part of the Navy in all our wars, and taking an especial pride in being fully prepared to perform creditable service in the Navy whenever called upon, the officers and men of the Coast Guard are inspired not only by the high tradition and fine history of their own service, but also by the splendid traditions, history, and indoctrination of the U.S. Navy. They have thus two rich heritages to be proud of and two standards of the same lofty character to live up to."

12 "COAST GUARD *IS* JOINT"

CAPT Alexander J. Hindle Jr., USCG (Ret.)

Captain Hindle's December 1998 ***Proceedings*** article was the winner of USNI's Coast Guard Essay contest. "Coast Guard *Is* Joint" outlined the USCG's important contributions to the joint force before 9/11, and there were many. What made this article really stand out were all the areas where the USCG could become even more joint if given the adequate funding and personnel. There is lots of potential for more jointness, especially as the USCG acquires more modern platforms.

"COAST GUARD *IS* JOINT"

By CAPT Alexander J. Hindle Jr., USCG (Ret.),
U.S. Naval Institute *Proceedings*, (December 1998): 30–33.

The future of the U.S. armed forces increasingly is joint. The landmark document *Joint Vision 2010* and its supporting publication, *Concept for Future Joint Operations*, lay out the rationale for this assertion. The 1997 National Military Strategy echoes the requirement that the services, explicitly including the U.S. Coast Guard, must be interoperable—institutionally, organizationally, intellectually, and systemically—to field the full-spectrum force required to meet the challenges of the 21st century.[1] The December 1997 report of the National Defense Panel notes that "all operations will be increasingly joint, combined, and interagency."[2] The implications for the Coast Guard should be apparent. Its relevance as a major contributor to the national security of the nation lies in its ability to be joint.

Indeed, the Coast Guard widely is recognized as a member of the joint community through simple but important things such as the Coast Guard seal appearing on joint publications, the display of the Coast Guard flag alongside those of the other services, and the inclusion of the Coast Guard in military recruiting advertisements. In addition, several Coast Guard manuals have been promulgated as joint publications, and Coast Guard ships and planes are included in joint capabilities reference materials. The Pentagon and the unified commanders welcome the inclusion of Coast Guard officers on their staffs and generally seek an increase in that presence. The demand for Coast Guard participation in joint exercises and operations exceeds the ability to meet it. At issue is whether the current level of effort will be enough to meet the demands of joint interoperability in the 21st century. The service needs to consider how much additional emphasis it should place on jointness.

First, a qualifier: By "joint" when talking about the Coast Guard, we do not mean joint in the sense of the Goldwater-Nichols Act (Defense Reorganization Act of 1986). The Coast Guard is not a Department of Defense (DoD) military service, and that statute does not apply to it. However, the objectives inherent in Goldwater-Nichols are just as applicable to the Coast Guard as to its sister services, especially because the Coast Guard becomes a specialized service within the Navy during times of war or when directed by the president.

What is meant by Coast Guard jointness is day-to-day interoperability and unity of effort with DoD. It means that the Coast Guard consciously and aggressively establishes as much common ground with DoD as feasible. Jointness, however, does not mean that the Coast Guard should lose its unique identity as a military service and federal agency, but rather that there are benefits for all involved if the Coast Guard seeks to maximize its joint identity.

Coast Guard jointness underscores the service's military nature as a fundamental, enduring, and defining characteristic of the organization. Without the military framework, the Coast Guard would be just another federal agency—a small one at that—performing a multitude of disparate functions, most of which could be performed by other agencies. In a classic example of the whole being greater than the sum of the parts, the Coast Guard uses its military essence to provide an effective, efficient multimission service for the American people.

Coast Guard jointness ensures the service interoperability that has enabled the Coast Guard to participate successfully in high-profile events, such as the Cuban and Haitian operations of 1994, the 1996 response to the Brothers to the Rescue shootdown in the straits of Florida, and the 1996 TWA Flight 800 response. Jointness is the lubricant that allows such operations to proceed smoothly, that allows the Coast Guard to call upon the support of the other services when needed. The enablers of this interoperability are the common language, standards, and doctrine of jointness. Even though the Coast Guard often is first on scene during natural disasters or national security concerns, it frequently lacks the capacity to complete the mission alone. Without the capability of achieving timely and effective interoperability, the ability of the Coast Guard to perform in a crisis would be endangered, and along with that, its raison d'être.

Other factors are involved, but this operational success wrought by joint interoperability was instrumental in bringing the Coast Guard (relative) fiscal success in the difficult budgetary atmosphere of the mid-1990s. The service is ready to meet the millennium largely intact, although reduced in personnel strength by approximately 10% compared to the start of the 1990s. The annual infusion of $300 million from DoD into the Coast Guard budget, upon which the service depends, arguably is contingent on Coast Guard jointness. Jointness also provides the Coast Guard with benefits in acquisition, personnel, and infrastructure support, and helps Coast Guard personnel receive equal treatment in legislation addressing military benefits.

What Does the Coast Guard Bring to Jointness?

The Coast Guard provides a relevant, non-redundant, and complementary military capability. While its warfighting capabilities are modest, it does fill a niche in the maritime arena that is likely to expand as a shrinking U.S. Navy concentrates its assets in high-capability ships. Then–Vice Admiral James M. Loy pointed out that a projected fleet of a new class of "maritime security" cutters could represent a sizable portion of the nation's naval force by 2020.[3] In September 1998, the Navy and Coast Guard signed a memorandum of agreement that committed the two services to cooperate in the development of a national fleet of future ships and cutters. The Coast Guard's "acceptable presence" around the world, created by its humanitarian missions, also provides the State Department and DoD with a useful maritime tool in cases where a gray hull or fuselage might not be welcome. Several Unified Commanders-in-Chief (CinCs) have recognized this and have used the Coast Guard to help shape the peacetime environments in their areas of responsibility.

The National Military Strategy, along with the National Defense Panel report, envisions increased interagency operations for the military services. The Coast Guard can assist DoD in dealing with other agencies as it addresses new, nontraditional threats under the broadening concept of national security. The Coast Guard has extensive experience in dealing with the civil sector on domestic issues with which the other services may be coming to grips for the first time. For example, the Coast Guard makes extensive use of the Incident Command System, a command-and-control arrangement widely used at all levels of the public and private sectors and which DoD is likely to encounter increasingly in future interagency operations.

What "Purple Work" Is the Coast Guard Doing?

At present the Coast Guard makes modest contributions of its assets to various joint operations and has been, upon occasion, the supported joint force commander. Recent examples of joint operations include Operations Desert Shield and Desert Storm, Haitian embargo operations, Haitian and Cuban mass migrations, Operation Uphold Democracy in Haiti, and Cuban Freedom

Flotilla events. In addition, Coast Guard cutters and aircraft regularly are provided for Joint Interagency Task Force (JIATF) operations, and the service has deployed cutters to Europe in support of U.S. European Command initiatives with Baltic, Mediterranean, and Black Sea nations. High-endurance cutters have deployed to the Arabian Gulf in support of the U.S. Central Command, and maritime law-enforcement detachments (LEDets) assist in the enforcement of the Iraqi embargo. The Coast Guard has made similar contributions to Operation Sharp Guard in the Adriatic. Cutters, port-security units, and Coast Guard/Navy harbor defense commands are written into the contingency plans of the warfighting CinCs. In addition, Coast Guard assets regularly participate in a wide variety of joint exercises.

More than 55% of the Coast Guard's liaison billets can be characterized as joint or interagency billets. Another 25% of the billets are assigned with the Navy, and most of them enjoy some degree of wider joint exposure. Key among the external assignments are the Coast Guard flag officers assigned as commanders of JIATFs East and West. Other joint assignments are the captains assigned to the unified CinCs, the Pentagon Joint Staff, and the Secretary of Defense Strategic Study Group. A commander is well placed in the Pentagon Joint Doctrine Division (J-7).

The Coast Guard assigns only a select few of its senior officers to joint senior services schools. Five senior officers are sent each year to joint courses at the National War College and Industrial College of the Armed Forces. An additional six commanders are sent to the Army, Air, and Naval War Colleges for the senior courses, where they receive valuable exposure to joint issues.

The Coast Guard has been actively involved with the Pentagon process that is expanding upon the concepts in *Joint Vision 2010.* The Coast Guard Director of Operations Policy is a member of the flag-level Joint Vision Working Group that is overseeing the process. Other representatives from Coast Guard Headquarters attend meetings of the Coordinating Authorities that are addressing the new operational and enabling concepts of *Joint Vision 2010.*[4] The Coast Guard's vision document, *Coast Guard 2020: Ready Today . . . Preparing for Tomorrow,* published in May 1998, parallels the thrust of *Joint Vision 2010.*

How Could the Coast Guard Be More Purple?

The Coast Guard already does a great deal in the area of military jointness, but will current levels be adequate for the future? If predictions of increased joint operations prove to be true, more jointness will be required of the Coast Guard. Progress is possible in the following areas:

Joint Operations. The single greatest contribution the Coast Guard can make to jointness is perhaps its most difficult to deliver. The demand for Coast Guard assets regularly outstrips available resources. Nonetheless, the Coast Guard must be as responsive as possible to requests from the joint community for personnel, aircraft, and cutters. Coast Guard leadership must be prepared to address the political questions that often accompany such use of Coast Guard assets. Area commanders should ensure that their force allocation models include appropriate weighting for joint operations and exercise requests. They should be prepared to make directed asset allocations to joint exercises and operations if necessary.

Joint Experimentation. Under a charter from the Secretary of Defense, Commander-in-Chief, U.S. Atlantic Command (CinCUSACom), has assumed responsibility for joint experimentation, which includes the *Joint Vision 2010* implementation process. The Coast Guard is being provided the opportunity to participate in joint experimentation, as it was for *Joint Vision 2010.* The Coast Guard should develop concepts of how it could employ its capabilities in support of future joint force commanders. These concepts should be offered to CinCUSACom as candidates for joint experimentation. The Coast Guard also should be prepared to make a commitment of resources to joint experimentation field exercises when the opportunity arises.

Defense of the Homeland. The NDP report places great emphasis on homeland defense as a 21st-century security challenge. If the nation's leadership adopts that strategy, the door effectively will have been opened for the Coast Guard and Navy to revisit the coastal defense role embodied in the maritime defense zone (MDZ) mission. The domestic MDZ role largely has been shelved in favor of an expeditionary harbor-defense command role in support of the warfighting CinCs. The defense-of-the-homeland concept offers the Coast Guard an outstanding opportunity to demonstrate its jointness and interagency interoperability. The Coast Guard should use the Navy/Coast Guard Board to explore the role of the MDZs under the emerging defense-of-the-homeland concept.

Coordination of Efforts. For much of its history, the Coast Guard conducted independent unit operations. However, as the nature of its missions evolved over the past 20 years, the ability of the service to work alone has dissipated. Operations such as drug and alien interdiction must be conducted in concert with DoD and other agencies to be effective. Nonetheless, the Coast Guard sometimes still fails to appreciate the interest that the CinCs have in its operations within their areas of responsibility. Conversely, the CinCs sometimes fail to understand that the Coast Guard may have legitimate missions in its areas of responsibility outside of DoD purview. The Coast Guard should, in accordance with the recommendation of the National Defense Panel report, more closely couple its international activities with the CinCs' regional stability programs.[5]

Joint Liaison Duty. The key to services' mutual understanding—the taproot of jointness—is effective liaison. But within the Coast Guard, liaison duty has a schizophrenic cast: the service trumpets the importance of such duty, but sends entirely different signals when the performance of the officers in liaison billets apparently is discounted by promotion selection boards. Consequently, such assignments often are undertaken with a great deal of trepidation by members of the officer corps. Other oddities of Coast Guard liaison duty are the unrealistic expectations the service has about what the assigned officers can accomplish. Commanders and below assigned to liaison duty are likely to wind up as staff officers. If the Coast Guard wants true liaison officers—unburdened by action-officer duties—it must assign captains. Conversely, it must accept the idea that a cost of jointness is the assignment of personnel to action-officer status who will do "purple work" that may have no direct connection to day-to-day Coast Guard business.

The Coast Guard must leverage joint billets to extract the maximum benefit to the service by assigning officers of the appropriate grade. The Coast Guard needs to understand the differences among action-officer, liaison, and special-program billets and develop memoranda of agreement for each billet to provide a common basis of understanding about the billet's responsibilities. It should increase the attractiveness of joint duty by ensuring that promotional and other selection panels understand the value of the contributions of joint-duty officers.

Joint Education. Understanding joint issues is an appropriate professional development requirement for Coast Guard leaders. Generally, it takes the assignment of a Coast Guard member to a billet that exposes the person to joint issues and operations for that member to realize the value of jointness to the Coast Guard. The service would be well served in having a larger portion of its ranks conversant on joint issues, which would enhance the Coast Guard's ability to function in the joint arena. The fact that the Coast Guard has joint responsibilities is something that should be impressed upon the officer corps at the points of accession. In addition, the Coast Guard Leadership Development Center should include Coast Guard jointness in the assortment of courses that will be taught. The Center should also add *Joint Force Quarterly* magazine to its suggested leadership reading list for middle- and senior-grade officers and senior enlisted. Also, the service is forgoing an opportunity to expand its cadre of joint-trained officers by not availing itself of the Armed Forces Staff College. The Coast Guard should reprogram a billet for the instructor staff at the Armed Forces Staff College, as that apparently is the quid pro quo for the Coast Guard to resume sending students to the school.

Doctrine. The Coast Guard has been reluctant to codify its procedures in doctrine, despite the existence of numerous internal directives and manuals that prescribe how it shall conduct its business. In addition to its internal value, doctrine would help define the capabilities of the Coast Guard for the other services, facilitating joint planning at the operational and tactical levels. The common misconception is that "doctrine is dogma," and that by formalizing doctrine, the flexibility and adaptability for which the service is renowned would be lost. However, doctrine—while authoritative—requires judgment in its application. The Coast Guard apparently has recognized this shortcoming, as a December 1997 message announced that it was developing handbooks for counterdrug and alien migration interdiction operations that would be published concurrently as Commandant Instructions and Naval Warfare Publications (NWPs). The Coast Guard has also begun to address the issue of doctrine with the ongoing development of Coast Guard Pub 1. This document will provide a common understanding of the fundamental principles and values that define its existence. The Coast Guard should undertake a program to systematically capture its operating principles and procedures in a formal body of doctrine. This is not a project that can be undertaken in the spare time of headquarters and area operations staffs. The best approach, in light of staffing and time constraints, would be to contract out the effort.

Flag Officer Visibility. The role of the flag corps is preeminent in firmly establishing the concept of Coast Guard jointness. The Coast Guard flag and senior executive service leadership should seize every photo opportunity to promote publicly the service's commitment to jointness. Recognizing that not every flag selectee may have had exposure to joint issues prior to selection, the Coast Guard should ensure that its new flag officers attend the Capstone Course prior to promotion or frocking.

Jointness can be expanded to the greater future benefit of the Coast Guard. As the Department of Defense studies and begins to shape its 21st-century future, the Coast Guard is in a position to influence those areas that will directly affect it. The value of the Coast Guard lies, in part, in its complementary and non-redundant contribution to national security—a role likely to grow in importance as the term "national security" comes to include matters beyond defense. However, the Coast Guard must seize the moment to solidify and expand upon its joint role in national security matters. Failure to do so will jeopardize the Coast Guard's role as a meaningful contributor to national security—and perhaps the Coast Guard's very existence.

Notes

1. Chairman, Joint Chiefs of Staff, *Shape, Respond, Prepare Now: A Military Strategy for a New Era*, September 1997, pp. 21–22.
2. Report of the National Defense Patrol, *Transforming Defense: National Security in the 21st Century*, available at www.dtic.mil/ndp (downloaded 2 December 1997), p. iii.
3. "Shaping Coast Guard Forces for Tomorrow's Challenges," presented 20 November 1997, sponsored by the Fletcher School, the Institute for Foreign Policy Analysis, Chief of Naval Operations, and Commandant of the Marine Corps.
4. Dominant Maneuver, Precision Engagement, Focused Logistics, and Full-Dimensional Protection enabled by Technological Innovation and Information Superiority.
5. NDP report, p. 32.

13 "HOMELAND SECURITY IS A COAST GUARD MISSION"

Stephen E. Flynn

Stephen Flynn is one of this nation's leading experts on homeland security. In a very prescient article, to say the least, Flynn submitted "Homeland Security Is a Coast Guard Mission" to the staff of *Proceedings* in July 2001 just months before 9/11. Moreover, Flynn's article provides a snapshot into the pre-9/11 policy food fights in Washington, D.C., which always left the U.S. Coast Guard underfunded. Finally, Flynn was right on target when he wrote, "The homeland security mission presents a historic opportunity for the U.S. Coast Guard to highlight the critical role it plays in the nation's defense."

"HOMELAND SECURITY IS A COAST GUARD MISSION"

By Stephen E. Flynn, U.S. Naval Institute *Proceedings* (October 2001): 72–75.

Homeland defense and homeland security have become the latest rage in commissions and think tanks around Washington. Over the past year, eight major studies and reports have rolled off the presses, sharing a remarkable degree of consensus. They agree that there is a real and imminent threat of a catastrophic attack on the American people and the critical infrastructure that is the backbone of our powerful society, and that the U.S. government is unprepared and possesses no adequate organizational structure to prevent or respond to such an attack. The Bush administration seems to be taking these findings to heart. In early May, Vice President Dick Cheney was tasked with overseeing the development of a coordinated national effort for protecting the nation against the use of weapons of mass destruction. At the Pentagon, a recent study prepared for the Secretary of Defense incorporates defense of the U.S. homeland into U.S. military strategy guidelines for the first time in decades.

The idea that we need to protect our homeland from attack does not sit well with most Americans. Ever since we won our national independence, we have enjoyed relative freedom from direct military threat, with the exception of some pesky Redcoats during the War of 1812 and Pancho Villa's incursions along the Southwest border at the start of the last century. But it's not just that our 21st-century adversaries may prefer to bring their battles to U.S. soil that makes us queasy. It also is a concern that the cure might be worse than the disease. Americans have never been enthusiastic about standing armies. In the post–World War II era, we accommodated ourselves to the need for a large national security establishment by clearly demarcating where its writ would run—overseas. We were willing to make an unparalleled investment to contain the Soviet Union and to deal with conflicts "over there." But the quid pro quo was supposed to be that civilians could enjoy their full freedoms here at home.

For many with memories of World War II, the surge in interest in homeland security undoubtedly conjures up images of enforced blackouts and armed beach and port security patrols. Those who lived through the first decades of the Cold War are likely to have flashbacks of air raid drills and backyard bomb shelters. For contemporary planners in the Pentagon, struggling to match paltry resources to growing missions, the increase in interest undoubtedly generates new anxieties that this will become an additional mandate that will distract them from their other important work.

The homeland security issue may generate uneasiness in many quarters, but it should not make the U.S. Coast Guard uneasy. Indeed, it would be a mistake for senior Coast Guard leaders to remain mute as this national debate unfolds. By stepping out smartly, the Coast Guard can both advance the service's interests and serve the American people.

The Terrorist Threat

As the world's predominant military, economic, and cultural power, the United States is "Public Enemy No. 1" for any group or nation that resents its global dominance. But terrorists, radical religious or ethnic sects, and rogue states who want to give form to their pique over the United States' unequaled global reach can hold few illusions about winning direct contests with U.S. military forces. Instead, the targets of tomorrow increasingly will lie in the civil realm, where the economic and cultural components of national power are vulnerable. The disturbing trends toward unconventional weapons proliferation—including nuclear, chemical, and biological weapons of mass destruction—portend that terrorists likely will have access to the means for conducting a catastrophic attack. In the largely unprotected ports, waterways, and coastal regions, there is ample opportunity to harm Americans, gain access to critical national infrastructure, and disrupt the nation's vital transportation lifelines.

The Bush administration appears poised to spend up to $100 billion to construct a national ballistic missile defense system, but officers and inspectors charged with policing the vessels and cargo moving to, from, and through U.S. ports and waterways know that it is not only the nation's aerospace that is wide open but its maritime space as well. Despite their best efforts over more than two decades, these inspectors have been able to interdict only a fraction of the illicit narcotics destined for our shores. Most ports have no security except that provided by minimum-pay private security guards hired by commercial tenants. The volume and velocity of people, cargo, and commercial and recreational traffic that move on the water far exceed the resources available for ensuring that these cross-border flows are complying with U.S. laws.

If an adversary wanted a weapon of mass destruction to reach the United States, he likely would consider the merits of transporting it on board a vessel or within a maritime container. When launched, a ballistic missile has a very pronounced signature, and the United States is capable of conducting a devastating retaliatory strike. So why would not an Osama bin Laden or some rogue state choose an alternative scenario, such as loading a chemical weapon into a container originating from a front company in Karachi, Pakistan, and ultimately destined for Newark, New Jersey? A terrorist might use a Pakistani exporter with an established record of trade in the United States. The container could have a global positioning system (GPS) device so it could be tracked as it moved through Singapore or Hong Kong to mingle with the more than half a million containers handled by each of these ports every month. It could arrive in the United States via Long Beach or Los Angeles and be loaded directly on a railcar for the transcontinental trip. Current regulations do not require an importer to file a cargo manifest with the U.S. Customs Service until the cargo reaches its "entry" port—in this case, Newark, 2,800 miles of U.S. territory away from where it first entered the country—and the importer is permitted 30 days' transit time to make the trip to the East Coast. When the container reaches the rail yard outside Chicago—which is one of the most important rail hubs in the United States—the weapon could be set off, long before its contents were even identified as having entered the country.

Most Americans and their defense planners are oblivious to just how open U.S. maritime borders are. If they were not, they likely would reconsider plans to spend so much on some rather fanciful technology against what most respected observers see as a very low-probability threat, and instead—or at least concurrently—would invest in lower-cost homeland security measures designed to prevent and protect against an attack by unconventional means.

The "weapon-in-a-container" scenario frames what is the essential challenge of homeland security. We must strike the optimal balance between permitting the free movements of legitimate travelers, cargo, and information, and advancing the capacity to identify and intercept illegitimate people and goods that would cause Americans harm. Pursuing the latter without being mindful of the former is not an option. Measures that would sacrifice freedom for the sake of security essentially are un-American, and sustaining U.S. economic competitiveness in a world where 95% of the consumers and much of the raw materials lie outside the United States requires that the barriers associated with conducting global business be kept to a minimum.

Anomaly Detection

Because striving for a failsafe system to protect the U.S. homeland is both unrealistic and likely to be counterproductive, does this mean that the only alternative is to stand by for globalization's heavy rolls? No. The best way to balance the imperatives of openness and control is to embrace a risk management approach. Risk management involves developing the means to identify transnational activities and actors that pose little or no risk to the United States so that limited regulatory, enforcement, and security resources can be targeted at those that present a high risk.

With so much of the world's trade moving by sea, and with so many vessels engaged in both work and play transiting along U.S. maritime frontiers, managing risk within the nation's largely open maritime space is no simple task. In 2000, 5.8 million 40-foot maritime containers and 211,000 commercial vessels entered U.S. ports, most registered under foreign flags. On the Great Lakes alone there are more than 4 million U.S.-registered small boats. How is it possible to filter the bad from the good given such numbers? The answer lies in anomaly detection, a relatively new concept being promoted by cybersecurity experts that most seasoned Coast Guard boarding officers and Customs inspectors have been practicing for a long time.

In the computer industry, anomaly detection is the most promising means for detecting hackers intent on stealing data or transmitting computer viruses. The process involves monitoring the flows of computer traffic with an eye toward discerning normal traffic that moves by way of the most technologically rational route. Once this baseline is established, software is written to detect aberrant traffic. A good computer hacker will try to look as much as possible like a legitimate user. But because he is not legitimate, he inevitably must do some things differently. Good cybersecurity software will detect that variation and deny access. For those hackers who manage to get through, their breach is identified and shared so that this abnormal behavior can be removed from the guidance of what is normal and acceptable.

In much the same way, the overwhelming majority of the vessels, people, and cargo that move in and out of our waters—particularly those originating in overseas ports—move in predictable patterns. If we have the means to track these flows, we will have the means to detect aberrant behavior. This is what happens when a Coast Guard boarding officer climbs on board a fishing vessel and discovers that it has the wrong kind of gear for the fishery in which the captain claims he is working. Anomaly detection within the maritime space is possible if the regulatory and enforcement agencies whose daily tasks place them in that space are given access to intelligence about real or suspected threats or are provided the means to gather, share, and mine data that provide a comprehensive picture of normal maritime traffic, to enhance their odds of detecting threats when they materialize. Coast Guard Commandant Admiral James Loy calls this "maritime domain awareness." Around Washington, he has been making the case that the nation needs this kind of capability. Through his advocacy, he also has been demonstrating that the Coast Guard is well positioned to play a leadership role in developing it.

Of course, possessing the means to detect a threat within the maritime domain is only the first step. The nation must also have the means to intercept that threat and exercise law enforcement action. A busy waterfront pier in Los Angeles or Seattle is hardly an optimal place to find and defuse a bomb. A better approach would be to intercept the vessel carrying the weapon offshore. If a shoreside evolution is required, the vessel could be escorted to a less vulnerable locale. For this kind of mission, the country would want a fleet of modern, swift, and capable cutters that can safely operate on the high seas, in all types of weather, deploying helicopters and small boats to transport boarding teams, night or day, while communicating securely with the National Command Authority.

Around the clock, 365 days a year, the Coast Guard is patrolling our nation's waterways, coastal regions, and exclusive economic zones, and operating far from our shores when the missions require. But increasingly the service performs its missions with platforms that are well past their useful service lives and kept operational only by constant repairs, thereby robbing an already austere operating budget. The service's Deepwater acquisition properly aims to rectify this unsustainable situation so that the United States will have the kind of maritime interception and law enforcement capabilities it needs to stop threats to the homeland before they arrive.

Because a terrorist still may succeed at evading good intelligence, detection, and interception assets, the final pieces to the homeland security mission are protection of critical infrastructure and the management of the consequences of an attack. The extent to which ports are critical infrastructure is highlighted by the dependency of California on a single pier in the Port of Long Beach for the offloading of 45% of all the maritime crude shipments (408,000 barrels per day) or roughly 25% of all the crude oil consumed by the state. Because California's gasoline refineries are all operating at full capacity, at any given time there is only enough oil stored in the region to supply them for two days. Accordingly, if the kind of terrorist attack that was conducted in Yemen against the USS *Cole* (DD-67) took place against a tanker tied up to that one pier, the economy of Southern California—which is bigger than the economies of most of the world's nations—would grind to a halt within a matter of days. Given such an attractive and almost completely unprotected target, a terrorist might prefer to attack that pier at Long Beach rather than a Navy frigate tied up at the San Diego Naval Base.

Coast Guard captains of the port will have an increasingly important role to play in gathering data to support intelligence collection efforts, conducting vulnerability assessments, raising awareness about those vulnerabilities, and leading local, state, and federal efforts designed to make ports more secure. These protective measures should help reduce the consequences of a terrorist incident within a U.S. port, but there would be consequences nonetheless. Coast Guard shoreside and afloat assets will play the role of first responder, as well as help manage the aftermath as the on-scene federal incident coordinator.

A Coast Guard Opportunity

The homeland security mission presents a historic opportunity for the U.S. Coast Guard to highlight the critical role it plays in the nation's defense. The nature of that mission goes well beyond the warfighting potential of the service's port security units and larger cutters, drawing on the entire tapestry of Coast Guard missions and capabilities. The most astute eyes and ears within the maritime domain belong to Coast Guard men and women doing their day-to-day missions. Whether conducting boating safety, marine and harbor safety, and fisheries patrols, or monitoring and working within our nation's waterways on a buoy tender or in a vessel traffic system, these personnel are positioned to detect aberrant activities that can pinpoint a terrorist threat. The service's work in support of migrant and drug interdiction provides it with many of the means to share information in the interagency process. Its long-standing relationships with the Navy and the Department of Defense make it an ideal go-between among the national security, law enforcement, and regulatory worlds. The work of Coast Guard marine safety offices provides an entrée to the maritime industry, port authorities, and local and state officials, which is essential for advancing critical infrastructure protection and consequence management within our nation's seaports. And the Coast Guard's superb international reputation can support necessary overseas efforts to improve security- and information-sharing arrangements that can reduce the risk that the world's maritime transportation system will be exploited by terrorists to hurt Americans at home. No matter how large an investment is made to reinvent the U.S. national intelligence and defense establishment for the post–Cold War world, it will be unable to duplicate the kinds of capabilities that the Coast Guard brings to the table.

The appeal of the Coast Guard's low-cost, multimission platforms coupled with its unique civil-military attributes make capitalizing on the Coast Guard as a lead agency for the homeland security mission an idea whose time has arrived. These attributes have the potential for real political resonance as the national missile defense and homeland defense debates unfold. There are many inside the D.C. beltway who have misgivings about the huge investment, the abandonment of the Anti-Ballistic Missile Treaty, and the consequence for U.S.

relations with Russia, China, and our European allies that missile defense entails. There also are those who have understandable reservations about assigning the U.S. military and national intelligence establishment a prominent role in domestic security. Collectively, these politicians and commentators are in search of alternatives that address their concerns without allowing their critics to portray them as weak on defense. A compelling alternative is a homeland security strategy that emphasizes a risk and consequence management approach, enlisting the unique capabilities of the U.S. Coast Guard and other agencies with border-management responsibilities.

14 "INTERNATIONAL WATERS, ILLICIT TRAFFIC"

CAPT Douglas M. Fears, USCG

Stopping the flow of illegal drugs via the maritime arena is one of the most important law enforcement missions carried out by the USCG. Captain Doug Fears, USCG, former U.S. Coast Guard Chief of Law Enforcement, provides a sneak peek into the USCG's War on Drugs in this August 2012 *Proceedings* article. The figures provided by Captain Fears on the amount of cocaine are just staggering. Given the fact that there are too few USCG assets to interdict the illegal drugs in the transit zones, it is amazing that the USCG has interdicted as much as it has done. One can only imagine how much more cocaine could be interdicted if the USCG was fully modernized and expanded to meet the threat posed by transnational criminal organizations.

"INTERNATIONAL WATERS, ILLICIT TRAFFIC"

By CAPT Douglas M. Fears, USCG, U.S. Naval Institute *Proceedings* (August 2012): 44–49.

The equation is simple: *Effective maritime interdiction = framework + assets + surveillance + intelligence.* Having an effective maritime-interdiction capability is a core national-security interest. Given the interconnectivity of the global supply chain, all nations are sustained and enriched by overseas trade within which illicit trafficking often hides in plain sight. Since its founding in 1790, the U.S. Coast Guard has been effectively conducting high-seas maritime interdiction, a seminal mission that has continued to evolve.

To support that capability, the need for investment in ships, maritime-patrol aircraft, and intelligence is reasonably well understood. However, few comprehend the maritime-interdiction framework. To most, it seemingly serves only a very narrow interest. Since the national-security value of maritime interdiction is not always apparent, it is helpful to consider it in a broader context. The maritime cocaine-interdiction framework is a useful case study in this regard.

High-Seas Cocaine—Stopping It En Masse

The Western Hemisphere Drug Transit Zone (WHDTZ) is an area roughly two times the size of the continental United States between the source and target countries of the cocaine trade. Maritime interdiction in this region is conducted in a highly developed manner, and it is the most effective way to remove the largest and purest quantities of cocaine before the drug comes ashore in Central America to begin its toxic land journey to North America.

Arresting illicit trafficking in the maritime approaches to the Americas is of vital strategic interest and critical to the ongoing investigatory focus to dismantle transnational criminal organizations. These criminals routinely and resiliently adapt their trafficking routes and methods to evade evolving enforcement efforts; this cat-and-mouse interaction will never cease. Therefore it must be perpetually managed. That requires the continual maturing of each element of the interdiction framework. The smuggling of cocaine has created an ever-increasing corrosive effect on all societies throughout the source, transit, and arrival countries. This corrosion is manifest in the pliancy of criminal organizations, associated violence, rampant corruption, proliferation of weapons, erosion of sovereignty, and deterioration of societal fabric, ultimately resulting in a downward spiral of hemispheric security. Curtailing the flow of cocaine is therefore key.

In simple terms, consider that supply reduction is a three-legged stool—targeting of criminal organizations, interdictions, and crop eradication. This article focuses on the interdiction leg, specifically, maritime interdiction—the most effective way to remove the largest quantities of cocaine at their highest levels of purity.

Furthermore, consider that maritime interdiction itself is also a three-legged stool—surface interdiction assets, maritime-patrol aircraft, and actionable intelligence. Decades into its maturing process, the counter-drug framework is an effective model for interdicting any maritime illicit traffic, in any of the global maritime commons. And while interdiction is a subset of the broader cocaine supply-reduction strategy, it is nevertheless a foundational component.

Not All Zones Are Created Equal

The geographic layers employed in the maritime halting of illicit traffickers could be described as the *departure zone* from the source country, the *transit zone* between the source and target countries, and the *arrival zone* of the target country. While there are some exceptions, the departure zone is largely an area of the source country's coastline and territorial seas, typically patrolled by the source country's naval or law-enforcement forces. Similarly, the arrival zone is patrolled by the target country's forces. In the case of the United States, it is patrolled by various federal maritime forces within the territorial seas (12 nautical miles from shore), and within state waters (generally 3 nautical miles from shore) where additional state and local forces patrol and interdict suspect vessels. The Coast Guard is the sole U.S. force with the authority to conduct maritime law-enforcement interdiction operations in international waters (from the U.S. 12-mile limit to the territorial sea of another nation), which is why Coast Guard cutters operate forward-deployed, days and weeks from land.

The departure and arrival zones are much more straightforward operating areas in terms of authorities and jurisdiction. And the capability and capacity of interdiction forces in these comparatively small areas are less costly, as forces can be dispatched based on an intelligence queue or short-distance routine patrol using short-range boats and maritime aircraft.

But between departure zone and arrival zone lies the transit zone—a vast area covering millions of square nautical miles. In these international waters, few forces have the combined authority, capability, and capacity to interdict traffickers. Hence, maritime nations must employ a cooperative framework for all aspects of the continuum, including the operational functions of detection, monitoring, interdiction, and apprehension.

Routine maritime patrol in the sprawling WHDTZ requires a significant investment in ships and maritime-patrol aircraft capable of operating hundreds or thousands of miles from land for extended periods, and in weather conditions that can turn from calm to extreme in a matter of days or even hours. Proponents of maritime domain awareness (MDA) as sole elixir for the presence of law-enforcement forces on the high seas are shortsighted. Knowing that illicit trafficking is under way in a gigantic space is not an adequate surrogate for having persistent presence on a threat-vector at sea. As Admiral Mike Mullen, the former Chief of Naval Operations and Chairman of the Joint Chiefs of Staff, stated in a 2005 speech at the National Defense University, "We hear a lot about virtual presence today. I believe that for a naval force, virtual presence is actual absence, and that simply won't suffice in the world in which we live." Only the persistent presence of high-seas law-enforcement capability *supported* by MDA makes effective maritime interdiction possible.

Such persistent presence of maritime-interdiction forces—in international waters, on known illicit-trafficking vectors—allows the capability to be coupled with actionable intelligence to overcome the tyranny of distance for the best results.

The Threat and the Playing Field

Why does maritime interdiction and removal matter? In rough numbers, consider the following:

- Approximately 1,000 metric tons of high-purity cocaine flow through the maritime WHDTZ every year.
- About 95 percent of all cocaine in transit from the source countries in South America's Andean region is in the maritime environment at some point in transit. Less than 5 percent of all cocaine that enters the United States does so by maritime conveyance.

- Cocaine purity is at its greatest in the maritime drug-transit zone—approximately 75 percent purity in the Caribbean Sea and eastern Pacific Ocean compared with 40 to 50 percent in the average North American city.
- The five-year average of cocaine removed in the WHDTZ by U.S. maritime forces is in excess of 100 metric tons per year. Partner-nation navies and coast guards collaborate on the removal of an additional 100 metric tons per year.
- The five-year average of cocaine interdicted at the U.S. Southwest border is in excess of 20 metric tons per year.
- The five-year average of cocaine interdicted across the continental United States is in excess of 25 metric tons per year.

In summary, much more cocaine volume, at higher purity levels, is interdicted in the maritime WHDTZ than in the entire maritime arrival zone and land interdictions in North America combined. The logical question is: How do we increase performance in WHDTZ maritime drug interdictions? Continuing to invest in our interdiction-framework relationships, in conjunction with the addition of more ships, maritime-patrol aircraft, and intelligence, in proportion to one another, will increase performance. All other contributions would be marginal.

While the removal of cocaine in the WHDTZ in the western Caribbean Sea and eastern Pacific is the center of gravity for cocaine interdiction, it is not simply about interdiction volume and purity of seized product. Cocaine is a toxin that comes ashore in the land-transit zone and fuels violence, corruption, and instability.

That instability is at the core of U.S. security interests in the region. Similarly, it is what our partners in Central America and Mexico fight every day for the continued existence of their proud ways of life and hopes for a peaceful and productive future. Effective maintenance of security can only be achieved by confronting the roots of the problem, while simultaneously continuing to invest in responsible governance, rule of law, and professionalization of law-enforcement forces. While the solution to all this is complex and very difficult to implement, the centerpiece of any successful outcome must include the interdiction of the largest, purest quantities of cocaine.

The Longest Arm of the Law

The U.S. Coast Guard has the broadest-reaching authorities of any U.S. maritime law-enforcement organization—perhaps of *any* law-enforcement organization. The Coast Guard is a U.S. military service, a U.S. law-enforcement agency, a full member of the intelligence community, and has its own investigatory service. It has 11 statutory missions carried out by a force of more than 40,000 personnel. This mixture of missions, functions, and authorities is unique in the U.S. government, and underpins the Coast Guard's operational maritime-interdiction success. Its broad law-enforcement and military authorities are what allow the Coast Guard to operate around the globe in direct support of U.S. sovereign interests. These authorities have allowed the Coast Guard to develop strong relationships with partner nations' enforcement and prosecutorial bodies to merge the sovereign interests of those countries and the United States through the use of bilateral law-enforcement agreements.

The Coast Guard is the U.S. government's executive agent for the execution and maintenance of maritime bilateral and multilateral law-enforcement agreements. In concert with the U.S. Departments of State and Justice, the Coast Guard maintains 45 such agreements and operational procedures, the majority of which are in the Western Hemisphere. While these agreements vary from country to country, based on each nation's constitutional and sovereign interests, they follow a similar model for coordinating maritime-interdiction activities. The agreements build on decades of operational experience and bilateral/multilateral relationships; furthermore, they contemplate what have become routine illicit-activity profiles (e.g., go-fast and semisubmersible trafficking profiles). The bilateral agreements are unique diplomatic instruments that were painstakingly negotiated and maintained to protect partner-nation constitutional and sovereignty issues, while creating a mechanism to facilitate operational cooperation and for partner nations to consent to prosecutorial action by the United States.

In naval terms, ship capabilities are typically described by their main batteries. The Coast Guard's "main battery" is the law-enforcement boarding team. A fully qualified boarding officer and his or her team carry combined law-enforcement and military authority, making them an adaptive force in both homeland-security and homeland-defense scenarios. There is simply no other service or agency in the U.S. government with such jurisdictional versatility that can be effectively deployed in the maritime commons.

The "Interdicted/Disrupted" Combo

While interdictions are important, it is also important to highlight a maritime-interdiction peculiarity, which is the jettisoning of cocaine. Traffickers often throw bales of cocaine overboard, or in the case of a self-propelled semisubmersible and other vessels in which the contraband is stored below decks, the entire load is scuttled with the vessel. The combination of the cocaine interdicted (seized) and the cocaine disrupted (jettisoned) is the total amount of cocaine removed from the smuggling pipeline. Perhaps the only land equivalent of removal would be if cocaine were lost in a fire immediately before it was seized. Nevertheless, three to four times more cocaine is removed by interdiction efforts in the WHDTZ each year than in all North American land interdictions combined.

Keeping the Team Rowing Together

The Maritime Operational Threat-Response (MOTR) Protocols were delineated in National Security Presidential Directive 41/Homeland Security Presidential Directive 13. Similar in history to the maritime bilateral agreements, the protocols were developed based on decades of maritime operational and interagency experience. The MOTR process is daily managed by the Global MOTR Coordination Center, an extremely effective, around-the-clock organization with the primary objective of convening all relevant U.S.-agency stakeholders to determine, in real time, a desired national outcome for maritime operational threats, from piracy to shipboard stowaways.

In the WHDTZ, cooperation is manifest in many different areas. The Defense Department, through the U.S. Southern Command and the Joint Interagency Task Force South (JIATF-S), has a mandate to oversee and coordinate the detection-and-monitoring (D&M) aspect of maritime trafficking. JIATF-S works closely with the Coast Guard's Seventh and Eleventh District commanders. The service oversees and executes the interdiction-and-apprehension (I&A) phase of maritime trafficking, as only the Coast Guard has the authority to interdict and apprehend suspect vessels and smugglers in international waters.

Additionally, the airborne contributions of Customs and Border Protection Air and Marine Branch are a vital and substantive part of the D&M phase of illicit maritime trafficking, many times vectoring in surface-interdiction assets for the endgame. In concert with the efforts of the U.S. Drug Enforcement Administration, Immigration and Customs Enforcement, and other key agencies, this combined effort is not only a model of cooperation, but also a force-multiplier in maritime-interdiction performance.

Partner-nation contributions are also vital. The Seventh and Eleventh Coast Guard District Command Centers, the JIATF-S Joint Operations Center, and each partner-nation operations center communicate tactical information routinely to facilitate maritime interdictions. In addition, partner nations regularly contribute resources to respond to identified threats as they are able.

Perfection in cooperation is never achieved. It requires routine interaction and periodic maintenance meetings for the bilateral agreements, to resolve differences and further refine procedures. Multilateral meetings allow the interdictors and prosecutors to share best practices and build trust.

Taking cooperation one step further, it is useful to have a structural relationship in maritime-interdiction operations that is directive in nature, with a clearly defined command authority. The Coast Guard and JIATF-S maintain operations-center-to-operations-center communications, shifting tactical control of interdiction assets depending on whether they're engaged in D&M or I&A operations. The seam between the two is managed daily through the ops-center relationships.

Cycle of Success

The interdiction would not be complete without the follow-on investigation and prosecution of the apprehended suspects. These efforts toward case closure are vitally important, using the fruits of the interdiction to further target the transnational criminal organizations and gain valuable intelligence that make future interdictions possible. The cycle-of-success concept is particularly important as it links all the seemingly pedestrian aspects of maritime interdiction, investigations, prosecutions, and intelligence into a strategically meaningful continuum. When all the contributing aspects are healthy, the cycle of success is healthy. Conversely, if any aspect of the cycle of success is in decline, the other aspects suffer.

The complexities of the maritime-interdiction framework are myriad. Approaching any maritime-interdiction problem, in any geographic area, must include many of the same elements employed in the WHDTZ example explored here. To operate successfully with limited resources, each aspect of this framework must be managed and maintained on a daily basis.

But the framework, whether applied in the WHDTZ or anywhere else in the global maritime commons, is meaningless without the ability and authority to project forces to an active threat-vector hundreds or thousands of miles from land.

An appropriate range of authorities exist, and our partnerships are cultivated daily; however, our nation needs continued investment in ships, aircraft, and maritime law-enforcement personnel. We are a maritime nation with a deteriorating and shrinking fleet of ships and maritime aircraft. We have a national-security investment choice to make—the impacts of which will have a noteworthy effect on our maritime-interdiction performance for decades.

15 "COAST GUARD INTELLIGENCE PROGRAM"

(Selection from chapter 25 of *The Coast Guardsman's Manual, 10th Edition*)

Jim Dolbow

Intelligence, while not one of the USCG's eleven statutory missions, nevertheless plays a key role in USCG operations. The USCG became a formal member of the U.S. Intelligence Community (USIC) on December 28, 2001. Chapter 25 of *The Coast Guardsman's Manual, 10th Edition*, details the extent of the USCG's intelligence enterprise from the tactical level all the way up to the strategic level. This selection is a must-read on the important role of intelligence in USCG operations as well as its unique military and law enforcement authorities.

"COAST GUARD INTELLIGENCE PROGRAM"

(Selection from chapter 25 of *The Coast Guardsman's Manual, 10th Edition*) by Jim Dolbow, (Naval Institute Press, 2013): 379–81.

The Coast Guard is singular among seventeen agencies that make up the Intelligence Community (IC) for its national and law enforcement intelligence statutory authorities in the maritime domain. Thus, the Coast Guard is uniquely positioned to provide actionable, timely, and fused intelligence to its operational commanders and IC partners. To assist in accomplishing the many diverse missions of the Coast Guard, senior leadership and operational commanders rely on the Coast Guard Intelligence and Criminal Investigations Program.

Because the Coast Guard employs unique expertise and capabilities in the maritime environment—in domestic ports, coastal waters, offshore regions, and even in foreign ports—where other U.S. Government agencies typically are not present, there exists the opportunity to collect intelligence that supports not only Coast Guard missions but other national security objectives as well.

The Coast Guard's Intelligence and Criminal Investigations Program includes its National Intelligence Element, the Criminal Investigations Service, the Counterintelligence Service, the Intelligence Coordination Center (ICC—the Coast Guard's production center), and the Cryptologic Service.

Its mission is to direct, coordinate, and oversee intelligence and investigative operations and activities that support all Coast Guard objectives by providing actionable (timely, accurate, and relevant) intelligence to strategic decision-makers, as well as operational and tactical commanders. The Coast Guard Intelligence and Criminal Investigations Enterprise also supports the National Strategy for Homeland Security and applicable national security objectives.

The Coast Guard has fully implemented rigorous policies and procedures to ensure compliance with the mandatory information-sharing provisions of Section 905(a) of the U.S.A. PATRIOT Act and Section 202 of the Homeland Security Act. It continues to capture and share law enforcement information that is relevant to homeland security and national security with the Department of Homeland Security, Intelligence and Analysis Directorate, and the Intelligence Community, where appropriate.

Support to Coast Guard operations is also bolstered with the following intelligence and law enforcement activities:

- Coast Guard Area Maritime Intelligence Fusion Centers (Pacific and Atlantic);
- Sector intelligence officers at twenty-six Coast Guard sectors;
- Field Intelligence Support Offices at Coast Guard sectors;

- COASTWATCH and Targeting Programs at the ICC;
- Global Maritime Intelligence Integration capability (partnering with the U.S. Navy and other key Intelligence Community members);
- Permanent presence on the FBI's National Joint Terrorism Task Force (JTTF) offices and ad hoc JTTFs providing a maritime nexus and expertise;
- Expanded participation in the Defense Attaché System that provides unique access to nontraditional foreign partners;
- National Tactical Integration Office—a Tactical Exploitation of National Capabilities (TENCAP)-like program that has increased the Coast Guard's maritime awareness in areas including fusion, identification of ships with imagery, anomaly detection, and information sharing;
- Operation Drydock, an interagency operation reviewing personnel holding Coast Guard-issued merchant mariner licenses and documents; and
- Project Scorpion, a national-level collaborative effort with the Departments of Justice, Defense, and Homeland Security to identify, track, and intercept aliens of interest with possible terrorist or affiliate ties before they arrive in the United States via maritime means.

16 "WORKING TOGETHER TO FREE WHALES"

CAPT W. Russell Webster, USCG

Protecting the lives of humpback whales is an example of the USCG's Living Marine Resources Enforcement (LMR) mission. Captain Webster's article was selected because it highlights the partnership between the USCG and the National Marine Fisheries Service. Moreover, whales are one of the most popular marine mammals in the world.

"WORKING TOGETHER TO FREE WHALES"

By CAPT W. Russell Webster, USCG, U.S. Naval Institute *Proceedings* (November 1999): 66–68.

In my time as commander of Coast Guard Group, Woods Hole, Massachusetts, I have come to appreciate that whales are a hot topic here on the Cape and in the Islands. People who have seen their local Coast Guard rescue stations downsized want to know how the Coast Guard can afford to devote resources to assist the Center for Coastal Studies (CCS) in disentangling right and humpback whales. And the people who are just interested in the process of whale disentanglement ask me how the Coast Guard and CCS work together to "free Willy."

The Resource Question

The answer to the resource question is simple in concept, but occasionally complex in the execution. The National Marine Fisheries Service (NMFS) is the federal agency responsible for the conservation and management of living marine resources. The Coast Guard assists NMFS in meeting management goals for protected marine mammals and has authority to perform certain law enforcement activities at sea. Barring a more urgent mission, such as life-saving search and rescue (SAR), the Coast Guard participates in these activities in fulfilling its role as a good steward of the ocean environment.

The same small coastal search-and-rescue stations, the Coast Guard Air Station at Otis, and several coastal patrol boats that perform about 1,500 rescue cases each year from Duxbury, Massachusetts, to Watch Hill, Rhode Island, also have assisted in disentangling at least 20 right and humpback whales over the past several years. Since 1994, Coast Guard commands have assisted CCS in surveilling, tracking, and responding to more than 55 whales reported to have been entangled. The Coast Guard and the National Marine Fisheries Service are responsible equally for enforcing the Endangered Species Act and the Marine Mammal Protection Act. In practice, however, the preservation of these large and rare mammals is a team effort among several agencies, including NMFS, CCS's Rapid Response Team, the Coast Guard, local harbormasters, and the Massachusetts Environmental Police, to name a few.

Freeing Whales

A 1998 rescue case might be the best way to answer the mail about how the Center for Coastal Studies and the Coast Guard work together to free whales. On 24 July 1998, responding to a report from a local harbormaster, the Coast Guard Cape Cod Canal Station notified CCS of a possible right whale entanglement.

By 1100, CCS had dispatched their R/V *Orion*, a Coast Guard Air Station HH-60 helicopter was in the air, and Station Cape Cod Canal had launched a 41-foot support boat. Flat, calm surface conditions near Cape Cod Canal, although ideal for boating, made whale sighting very difficult. The situation required close coordination, cooperation, and communication among the search, support, and rescue vessels and aircraft.

Finally, after locating the whales twice and losing sight of them both times, at 1420 CCS's team, with multiagency support vessels, was alongside the entangled whale. For nearly two hours, the CCS Rapid Response Team examined the lines wrapped tightly around the whale's flukes and attempted to slow the animal with a series of floats. Eventually, they were able to stop the whale by attaching a large sea drogue to the trailing gear. With the whale's forward motion impaired, the team was able to approach close enough to begin cutting away the gear. At about 1650, after 30 seconds of violent thrashing, the whale shook free of all of the lines and took off at high speed just beneath the surface. Researchers were able to identify the entangled whale as a six-year-old male last seen in the Bay of Fundy in September 1997, with the same gear wrapped around its tale and flukes.

The Center for Coastal Studies is the only agency authorized by NMFS to disentangle marine mammals on the East Coast. The Coast Guard in Woods Hole and CCS have been working together since 1994, and each agency contributes complementing resources to the total effort of whale sighting, tracking, and disentanglement. Coast Guard platforms, for example, typically have a greater cargo capacity than CCS's rapid-response chase boats, so the CCS's 1,500 pounds of response equipment is forward staged at several Coast Guard stations. This enables those assets with heavy-lift capability (Coast Guard boats and helicopters) to have ready access to the equipment needed by CCS, and enables CCS to focus on getting to the scene, knowing that their Coast Guard teammates are en route with the gear.

The Whale Disentanglement program has been expanded to include a multiagency Marine Mammal Surveillance program for Cape Cod Bay, launched in 1997, to include the aforementioned agencies and members of the U.S. Coast Guard Auxiliary, a civilian voluntary organization. When CCS needed help in quantifying the numbers, types, and locations of their customers—the whales—a large number of Coast Guard auxiliarists were trained to identify the different species and make reports in the standard NOAA format. Coast Guard auxiliarists also make patrols to the marine-life-rich Stellwagen Bank Sanctuary, [providing] knowledge that will help us better protect endangered right whales, other species, and the environment. The auxiliarists' air resources are used to patrol Stellwagen Bank, and auxiliarists now ride whale-watching boats in a formal observation program.

The efforts of Coast Guard units in northern waters have been hailed as exemplary, and these multiagency procedures are being considered for use in other Coast Guard districts in the southeastern United States and in Canada.

A Look Toward the Future

A 1988 NMFS workshop on whale watching—with participation by researchers, government officials, and industry representatives—recommended establishing minimum approach distances based on regional considerations (type species, location, habitat use, and behavior) that appear to influence whale reaction to vessels. For New England's whale-watching fleet, voluntary guidelines for safe operating procedures for maneuvering vessels near whales include no head-on approaches, no more than one vessel within 300 feet of a whale at any time, and a no-approach zone of 100 feet from a whale. By most accounts, local whale-watching companies have been vigilant in their self-policing actions.

Nevertheless, in January 1999, CCS and the Gerry E. Studds Stellwagen Bank National Marine Sanctuary cosponsored a forum at the Massachusetts Maritime Academy in Bourne to review NMFS's old whale-watching guidelines. Of particular interest were measures to protect the scarce northern right whale.

Right whale safety is complicated by that species' elevated mortality rate, which may result from "particular behavioral patterns, such as surface feeding or courtship activities, which render these animals vulnerable and/or unresponsive to approaching vessels." About 27% of known mortalities from western North Atlantic right whales have resulted from collisions with vessels. When one considers the small population of right whales—about 300—many argue that even one death is too many.

Of the many hundreds of whale-watching sorties in 1998, there were only two collisions with whales. The first occurred at fairly high speed. A conventionally powered, propeller-driven whale-watch vessel, operating in an area without a concentration of whales, apparently killed a minke whale. In the second case, a jet-powered (capable of high speeds) whale-watch vessel was proceeding slowly when it struck the whale, but the humpback survived despite the collision. This paradox highlights the illogicality of any discussion of speed limits near whales that does not also consider location as well as hull and propulsion designs. In addition, any restrictions on the speed of vessels near whales must be practical and enforceable.

The conventional standard for safety of speed at sea in international waters is prescribed in the International Collision Regulations: "Every vessel shall at all times proceed at a safe speed so that she can take proper and effective action to avoid collision and be stopped within a distance appropriate to the prevailing circumstances and conditions." Factors that should be considered include visibility, traffic density, maneuverability of the vessel, sea state, wind, current, and the vessel's draft.

Perhaps the Coast Guard's directions for their own cutters when operating in the vicinity of whales could become a standard. Coast Guard procedures call for cutters to "use caution and be alert for whales, using appropriate speed to reduce the possibility of whale strikes." When whale activity is at its peak in the Great South Channel and Cape Cod Bay, Coast Guard cutters post marine mammal–trained lookouts to watch for whales. According to David Mattila of CCS, "the guidelines are respected by the commercial whale-watching operators, but compliance may vary depending on whale abundance, time constraints, vessel operator, and/or weather. Disregard and/or ignorance of the guidelines by recreational boaters remains a serious problem, especially during peak summer periods."

In October 1998, Coast Guard units were mobilized to develop a whale reporting system with NMFS and NOAA to focus on merchant mariners operating merchant vessels greater than 300 gross tons. The International Maritime

Organization–approved system, which went into effect on 1 July 1999, requires "commercial ships entering known critical habitats such as the Great South Channel to call in their position before entering the area and to receive whale avoidance guidance." Coast Guard marine safety units also are delivering northern right whale educational packages to merchant vessels in East Coast ports.

The Coast Guard's Auxiliary also will provide whale educational training and information to recreational fishermen and boaters. A well-educated, sensitized community of whale-watching and merchant vessels is not enough, if unknowing recreational boaters run blindly among the endangered mammals.

As public concern for our nation's ocean resources grows, those who operate ships and enforce maritime laws will be asked to do more to protect that environment and to achieve the proper balance between resource use and species protection. The Coast Guard realizes the importance of this issue and is beginning to incorporate widespread, individual regional initiatives such as whale disentanglement and marine debris cleanup into a single strategy that will highlight the Coast Guard's role as a leader in protecting our marine ecosystems. This developing initiative, Campaign Ocean Steward, will further commit the Coast Guard, as we enter the 21st century, to being a good steward of the oceans.

17 "MORE ASSETS FOR THE ARCTIC"

CAPT Lawson Brigham, USCG (Ret.)

Icebreaking is one of the Coast Guard's most neglected missions. Captain Brigham was right on target advocating for more icebreakers to close the "Icebreaker Gap" in the Arctic in this December 2015 *Proceedings* article. The USCG has only two polar icebreakers, compared to more than forty Russian icebreakers.

"MORE ASSETS FOR THE ARCTIC"

By CAPT Lawson Brigham, USCG (Ret.), U.S. Naval Institute *Proceedings* (December 2015): 30–35.

By any measure 2015 was a challenging and highly successful year for U.S. Coast Guard polar operations and the nation's two polar icebreakers, the USCGC *Polar Star* (WAGB-10) and *Healy* (WAGB-20). Dialogue is continuing on how to rebuild the nation's polar icebreaker fleet, with President Barack Obama weighing in on the issue in September during his visit to Alaska and in a White House Fact Sheet announcing new federal Arctic investments, including icebreakers.[1] Likely not since the time of President Franklin D. Roosevelt's request during World War II for a U.S. icebreaker fleet has a U.S. president been personally and directly involved in such issues.[2]

Deployments to the polar ends of the world showcase today's global maritime reach of the United States provided by Coast Guard polar icebreakers. Recapping the operational year, the *Polar Star* and *Healy* supported multiple U.S. agencies in their polar work and a major international ocean-research program. A notable search-and-rescue operation was executed in a remote region with difficult Antarctic sea ice conditions. The *Healy* completed the first U.S. unaccompanied icebreaker transit to the North Pole as well as the cutter's third visit there, but the first since 2005. These highly successful operations in Antarctic waters and across the central Arctic Ocean basin visibly demonstrate how an effective icebreaker capacity can provide reliable and unambiguous U.S. polar maritime presence.

Unique National Maritime Assets

Coast Guard polar icebreakers are instruments of national policy and the visible, sovereign presence of the United States in Arctic and Antarctic waters. They are foremost capital maritime and naval assets of the U.S. government that historically have supported a host of federal agencies. Operating independently in the polar regions where the United States has broad national interests, these specialized naval vessels can provide the commander-in-chief and the unified combatant commanders—the Northern and Pacific Commands would be the obvious potential Department of Defense users—a unique polar capability that is undeniably an integral component of American naval and maritime power. No other surface ships in the U.S. National Fleet (a joint U.S. Navy and Coast Guard concept and effort to address commonality and interoperability) can operate safely and effectively anywhere on the global oceans and along the relatively uncharted coastal waters of the Arctic and Antarctic. Surface and subsurface combatants rarely operate in these high-risk and shallow coastal waters, making a Coast Guard icebreaker the sole U.S. maritime and naval presence in those areas.

A U.S. polar icebreaker must also be viewed as a Coast Guard cutter with an inherent design that allows effective operation in all types of sea ice, along with sustained on-scene presence and assured polar marine access. Cutters such as the *Polar Star* and *Healy* are essentially mobile Coast Guard multi-mission bases or platforms with long-range endurance in all polar marine regions. Ship-based mobility and the agility and flexibility to respond in the face of rapidly changing sea ice and other polar environmental conditions are an icebreaker's greatest assets.

A commanding officer of these ships holds a wide range of legal authorities and responsibilities identical to all Coast Guard cutter commanders. That same captain also leads an independent marine operation with all its logistical challenges to the far reaches of the planet, providing the United States with a key global maritime capability. Every officer who has served on board one of these cutters understands the singular importance of this strategic requirement. A review of the types of missions with which a captain might be tasked on a polar deployment is instructive. Several examples illustrate a complex suite of plausible missions:

- Conducting Coast Guard statutory missions (such as law enforcement; search and rescue; marine safety; marine environmental protection; aids to navigation; defense readiness; ports, waterways and coastal security; and more) in U.S. and international waters. Of importance, all cutters are the primary U.S. maritime law-enforcement presence at sea.
- Enforcing U.S. law and sovereign rights in the U.S. territorial sea, contiguous zone, and exclusive economic zone. Operations could include enforcing U.S. law on American vessels and citizens who might be operating in Antarctic waters for research, contract work, or adventure tourism.
- Responding to high-latitude incidents, emergencies, and potential maritime disasters from ships or marine operations associated with offshore development such as exploratory drilling. In such circumstances an icebreaker acts as the U.S. government's on-scene presence for command and control and can provide icebreaking in support of unlocking frozen harbors and waterways to facilitate commercial supply access.

- Conducting science and research in the national interest in the most demanding and remote regions at both ends of the world. Expeditions could include polar marine-transportation research and development in support of future systems for the U.S. maritime Arctic.
- Conducting bathymetric and scientific surveys north of Alaska to support a future U.S. extended continental shelf claim under the provisions of Article 76 of the United Nations Convention on the Law of the Sea, and more traditional bathymetric surveying along select routes within the U.S. maritime Arctic.
- Working in concert with U.S. and foreign polar research vessels and assuring access to remote survey locations that only a few of the world's icebreakers can reach.
- Serving as an integral element of a support and search-and-rescue network for U.S. naval operations and DoD research in the Arctic Ocean. Support to the DoD can include icebreaking operations along the western coast of Greenland to the U.S. northernmost defense facilities at Thule Air Base.
- Acting as a mobile observation platform in all polar marine environments and during long transits of the global ocean and providing ocean and atmospheric data to ground truth satellite and aerial observations. Support to such agencies as NOAA, the National Science Foundation (NSF), the National Air and Space Administration, and the DoD for polar environmental observation has been long-standing.
- Conducting icebreaking operations in support of the U.S. Antarctic Program, led by the NSF, such as the seasonal breakout of the McMurdo base for resupply-ship access and conducting Antarctic Treaty inspections around the continent led by the Department of State.

Notably, all of these missions have been conducted by Coast Guard polar icebreakers in recent decades during an era of fewer ships and an aging fleet. The current imperative to replace these capital assets is what the president addressed during his visit to Alaska. Announced were his plans to accelerate acquisition of additional icebreakers, with mention of a key caveat for multiple ships that can operate year-round in the Arctic Ocean.[3] This is a significant high-end operational requirement that suggests new icebreakers would be among the largest and most powerful afloat. Viewed from strategic and global perspectives, such ships could also conduct all current and future U.S. icebreaking requirements in the Antarctic.

Links to Arctic Marine Transportation

There is considerable misunderstanding about the future use of the Arctic Ocean for marine transportation and the potential role of icebreakers as facilitators of marine traffic. Using a scenarios or futures effort, the Arctic Council's Arctic Marine Shipping Assessment (AMSA), released in 2009, found that the primary driver for Arctic navigation is the development of onshore and offshore natural resources and many links to global commodities markets (and prices).[4] Another finding was that the profound Arctic sea ice retreat being observed in all seasons is important to navigation in that it provides greater marine access and potentially longer seasons of navigation.

However, also key is that the Arctic Ocean remains fully or partially ice-covered for nearly eight to nine months each year. It is not an ice-free ocean, and one plausible navigation season will likely be three to four months in summer along the entire length of the Northern Sea Route (NSR) from Kara Gate to the Bering Strait; year-round navigation has been maintained for more than three decades in the western areas of the Russian Arctic.[5]

In an effort to build a reliable and safe national Arctic waterway, Russia employs a fleet of large nuclear- and diesel-powered icebreakers for use in convoying and ice escort of commercial ships that are primarily carrying natural resources out of the Russian Arctic to global markets. However, even Russian maritime experts state that the NSR is a seasonal complement to a route using the Suez Canal around Eurasia.[6] Few believe the NSR will become a trans-Arctic container-shipping route, primarily [because it is] limited by its seasonality of access and overall environmental challenges that have an impact on reliability.[7]

Two highly relevant issues are influencing the possible operation of government-owned icebreakers for potential ice convoy in the Arctic marine areas of the United States and Canada. One issue is technical: the emergence of highly capable icebreaking commercial carriers that operate independently without the need for icebreaker escort. This is the likely future operational mode that is economically viable for commercial ships throughout the Arctic Ocean. These advanced icebreaking cargo ships have successfully sailed in the Russian maritime Arctic, including the NSR, and within the Canadian Arctic and through the Northwest Passage. The second issue relates to national policy and the future establishment of U.S. and Canadian Arctic marine transportation systems that could require escort or convoy icebreakers to extend the ice-navigation season beyond summer.

Would the two governments provide Coast Guard icebreakers for routine escort duties if many of the ships being supported do not trade in U.S. and Canadian ports? Such a scenario would seem problematic, and a viable alternative would be to have privately owned icebreakers chartered to support commercial shippers where and when required. While the justification of new U.S. Coast Guard icebreakers is clearly not based on convoying commercial ships in open Arctic seas, these ships would be available for response operations and potentially for the breakout of ports and coastal waterways (such as is conducted on the Great Lakes and in the U.S. northeast).

Past Polar Icebreaker Studies

In July 1984 the Coast Guard released a major interagency assessment, the *United States Polar Icebreaker Requirements Study* (*PIRS*), which had been mandated by the Office of Management and Budget.[8] This key analysis has remained a framework document on U.S. polar icebreaker issues for three decades. It provided the historical context for U.S. polar ships that have operated in Alaska since its purchase from Russia in 1867, in war-time theaters such as Greenland during World War II, and in the Antarctic since the early 20th century. The report affirmed the need to replace aging *Wind*-class icebreakers with new polar icebreakers operated by the Coast Guard.

A fleet of four icebreakers was recommended to meet a broad range of strategic and bipolar national interests. *PIRS* was updated in 1990 by a presidential report to Congress, which concluded that a fleet of the two *Polar*-class ships and an NSF polar research vessel should be joined by a new polar icebreaker with enhanced research capabilities. This report was the impetus for Congress to fund construction of the *Healy*, which was commissioned in 2000.

A high-level committee of the National Research Council released an authoritative and comprehensive study of future U.S. polar icebreaker needs in 2007.[9] It contains strong recommendations that the United States must continue an active and influential presence in the Arctic and Antarctic and maintain a fleet of Coast Guard polar icebreakers. Again, this study called for the renewal of the nation's polar icebreaker fleet.

In 2010 a report prepared for the Coast Guard by outside consultants—the *United States Coast Guard High Latitude Region Mission Analysis*, using operations-research modeling—concluded that to meet its statutory polar missions the service would require three heavy and three medium icebreakers. More ships would be needed (a mix of six heavy and four medium icebreakers) if a requirement for continuous polar presence was maintained, consistent with a joint Naval Operations Concept developed that year. The bottom line for all of these studies is the need for the U.S. government to operate a fleet of Coast Guard polar icebreakers to meet our broad national interests in the emerging Arctic and Antarctic. All of these studies are consistent in recommending three or more highly capable Coast Guard polar icebreakers for global operations.

Federal Budget Challenges

In an era of multiple congressional budget constraints, the funding for even a single new polar icebreaker (at $800–900 million) is complex. It has been very difficult for the administration and Congress to identify a viable and fundable long-term strategy for icebreaker procurement. A significant challenge the Coast Guard has confronted for decades, even when under the Department of Transportation, has been the size of its acquisition, construction, and improvements account. That cannot easily accommodate partial funding identified for a polar icebreaker, given the range of cutter, aircraft, and shoreside assets that require renewal and replacement.

The Coast Guard, with a strongly held view that a polar icebreaker is a national asset with multiple agency users, seeks to have significant funding contributions from other agencies. This could only come about by those agencies' deferral or cancellation of a host of future acquisitions such as aircraft, ships, weapons, satellites, research equipment, and more. It is important to remember that procurement of the *Healy* was accomplished with non–Coast Guard funding solely from the Navy's shipbuilding account. A more equitable strategy must be found. Others are pursuing alternative strategies to somehow reduce or defer funding for polar icebreakers:

- Funding the reactivation of the USCGC *Polar Sea* (WAGB-11) as a stopgap measure while new ships are under construction.
- Investigating strategies to build an icebreaker in a foreign shipyard (today likely illegal without presidential intervention, and doubtless politically unacceptable).
- Pursuit of leasing arrangements of polar icebreakers with the private sector (notably, the entire cost of a long-term federal lease must be identified up front; such leases are likely more expensive to the federal government and the taxpayer).

One plausible future strategy may be incremental increases in the Homeland Security/Coast Guard budget for icebreaker acquisition with costs spread over a broad suite of stakeholder agencies. This would surely require a directive from President Obama or his successor. Action even today would create a several-year gap in the operation of the nation's most capable icebreaker while awaiting the commissioning of a new ship.

Looking Forward

Multiple interagency, independent, and Coast Guard assessments—and more than three decades of debate—have highlighted the strategic needs for U.S.

government-owned polar icebreakers best operated by the Coast Guard. With a rapidly changing Arctic and rising marine use in the region, these requirements have increased, providing greater strategic clarity on this issue. The U.S. Arctic policy statement in 2009 and a *National Strategy for the Arctic Region* issued in 2013 have reinforced our national interests in the area. Most would agree that our national polar (maritime) interests are not well served by outsourcing them to foreign governments. Nor are these same strategic needs met by potentially available (but less capable) domestic or foreign-flag commercial icebreaking ships that lack the robust, multi-mission capacity of Coast Guard icebreakers.

The time for further study and continued debate about U.S. polar icebreakers is over, as surmised by President Obama and his Executive Office team, with action taken as far back as a Fiscal Year 2013 budget submission to initiate an icebreaker-procurement process. A "whole of government" approach responding to this deficit and funding these national assets is still required to harness interagency and congressional support and limit parochial interests and budgetary rivalry. A recent clarion call in Washington and the current U.S. chairmanship of the Arctic Council reminds Americans that we are an Arctic nation.

A strong signal is also needed to remind all of us that America, as a leading and influential polar nation, continues to have critical strategic interests and key investment needs in both polar regions throughout the 21st century. Few requirements are more important than modern Coast Guard icebreakers that maintain our *global* maritime capability, assure polar marine access, and provide visible, effective U.S. maritime presence.

Notes

1. "Fact Sheet: President Obama Announces New Investments to Enhance Safety and Security in the Changing Arctic," The White House, 1 September 2015, www.whitehouse.gov/the-press-office/2015/09/02/fact-sheet-president-obama-announces-new-investments-combat-climate.
2. *Polar Icebreakers in a Changing World: An Assessment of U.S. Needs* (Washington, D.C.: National Research Council of the National Academies, 2007), 54, www.nap.edu/read/11753/chapter/1.

3. "Fact Sheet: President Obama Announces New Investments." 1 September 2015.
4. Arctic Marine Shipping Assessment (Arctic Council, April 2009), www.pame.is.
5. CAPT Lawson W. Brigham, USCG (Ret.), "Russia Opens Its Maritime Arctic," U.S. Naval Institute *Proceedings* 137, no. 5 (May 2011): 50–55.
6. "Northern Sea Route Slated for Massive Growth," *The Moscow Times*, 4 June 2013, www.themoscowtimes.com/business/article/northern-sea-route-slated-for-massive-growth/481093.html.
7. Steven M. Carmel, "The Cold, Hard Realities of Arctic Shipping," U.S. Naval Institute *Proceedings* 139, no. 7 (July 2013): 38–41.
8. "United States Polar Icebreaker Requirements Study, Interagency Report," U.S. Coast Guard, Washington, D.C., 11 July 1984, www.nap.edu/read/11753/chapter/18#114.
9. *Polar Icebreakers in a Changing World: An Assessment of U.S. Needs*, 54.

18 "COAST GUARD IS A PARTNER IN CARIBBEAN SECURITY"

Eric Miller

Sam J. Tangredi, editor of a companion U.S. Naval Institute Wheel Book entitled *The U.S. Naval Institute on Naval Cooperation*, wrote: "International naval cooperation is not about building partnerships for partnerships' sake, but for building trust—the trust that results in greater interoperability and, at its most effective, a greater commitment to action. The more naval forces operate together, the more trust is (usually) generated. . . . We must understand how to manage international cooperation to gain its strategic benefits and avoid its lee shores."

Mr. Miller does an outstanding job discussing the role of the USCG in the Caribbean in his December 1999 *Proceedings* article entitled, "Coast Guard Is a Partner in Caribbean Security," which also received First Honorable Mention in the U.S. Naval Institute's Coast Guard essay contest. The USCG epitomizes partnership and sets the gold standard for the rest of the U.S. government.

"COAST GUARD IS A PARTNER IN CARIBBEAN SECURITY"

By Eric Miller, U.S. Naval Institute *Proceedings* (December 1999): 58–61.

The end of the Cold War and the continuing globalization of the world economy have greatly enhanced the importance of Latin America and the Caribbean to the United States. The relationship between the United States and the rest of the Western Hemisphere, articulated in the beginning of the 19th century by President James Monroe, often has been characterized by an imperial hubris that has placed the concerns of Washington over those of Western Hemispheric nations themselves. Moreover, the justification for questionable policies, such as repeated military interventions and political manipulation, rested largely on the overall interests and perceptions of the United States. Yet, as scholars herald the "end of history" and the apparent death of the great ideological battles (those between monarchism and republicanism, conservatism and liberalism, capitalism and socialism, and democracy and authoritarianism), it is now more possible than ever before to forge a greater sense of hemispheric community.[1]

For much of the Cold War, the United States focused on the security of the European continent, while encouraging greater economic and political integration of European states. Today, however, as the euro stands to challenge the U.S. dollar in the next century, U.S. policy makers realize that neglecting the Western Hemisphere, with its 800 million consumers and more than $10 trillion in national product per year, could prove disastrous. In the 1990s, U.S. policy evolved slowly, but it did begin to adapt to this growing shift in global priorities.

It was only in the last few years, coinciding with Peter F. Romero's appointment as acting assistant secretary of state for Western Hemisphere Affairs, that the rhetoric of U.S. policy changed accordingly. Romero has been outspoken as to the importance of Latin America and the Caribbean for U.S. interests. As Romero has stated on numerous occasions, at long last a "new partnership" among the many nations of the Western Hemisphere is possible with the hope of bringing about a heightened "sense of community."[2] With this new strategic vision, U.S. policy makers must find ways to foster cooperative ties. Implementing such a vision is infinitely complex, but small steps along the way can prove monumental in attaining greater hemispheric cooperation. A bold new commitment and imaginative diplomatic measures are required for this partnership to become reality.

The U.S. Coast Guard can serve these goals effectively and help build a genuine partnership, while solidifying its role as a unique and valued instrument of national security. Caribbean nations are highlighted in this discussion because the Coast Guard can play its greatest role in the development and support of smaller nations that pursue "inshore territorial defense navies" or "brown-water" maritime forces.[3]

From Soft Power to Hard Power

The Coast Guard can enhance the sovereignty and independence of the smaller Caribbean nations for several reasons, many of which reinforce one another. First, Caribbean nations look to the United States as a powerful and successful nation. In the past, this power has been exercised in ways that often undermined the sovereignty of Caribbean nations. Nonetheless, the allure of U.S. power remains quite compelling. The political scientist Joseph Nye coined the phrase "soft power" to describe the cultural allure of the United States, arguing that this was the primary characteristic that made the United States "bound to lead" in the world.[4] This is the case in the Caribbean since no other world power is as active in or important to the region as the United States.

Organizational theorists argue that new organizations often look to other well-established and successful organizations during their development. In the process, new organizations begin to look more and more like other organizations before them, a process called isomorphism. The logic is simple—new organizations find it prudent to adopt procedures and structures that have proved successful. To ignore the lessons learned by others would place younger organizations in jeopardy of replicating past failures. In this regard many Caribbean nations look to the United States for guidance, realizing that the institutional success of the Coast Guard can serve as a blueprint for their maritime development. The Coast Guard, for instance, remains the lead U.S. service for the Haiti Multiagency Maritime Initiative, which focuses on improving Haiti's maritime infrastructure and security.

Second, the Coast Guard makes a less intimidating military force than other branches of the armed services. Hands-on personal training, a reputation for humanitarian service, and the versatility to assist in any way possible are all characteristics that set it apart from the conventional military. Coast Guard ships are warmly received in most Caribbean ports because they do not represent U.S. power the same way Navy vessels do. As one senior Coast Guard officer stated, "[I]n particular our humanitarian nature as lifesavers, protectors of the environment, and the ability to help develop stronger economies make us a trusted partner. But, it is our people who develop this trust by training, working, and operating alongside foreign partners."[5]

The Coast Guard is also a more relevant model for developing maritime services in the Caribbean because of its relative numbers, size of vessels, multimission character, and humanitarian nature.[6] Many of the missions the Coast Guard faces are of paramount concern for the smaller Caribbean nations: fisheries and resource law enforcement, search and rescue, maritime interdiction, river and waterways management, port activities and maritime transportation safety, environmental safety and pollution control, and emergency response. The transnational character of threats in the Western Hemisphere further strengthens these mutual interests. Prominent among these threats are drug smuggling, illicit migration, gunrunning, illegal fishing, and environmental degradation. As Coast Guard Commandant Admiral Robert Kramek noted shortly after the May 1997 Caribbean Summit in Barbados, "we know the people, we know the geography, and, most importantly, we understand the maritime challenges that the Caribbean nations face."[7]

Beyond this convergence, the Coast Guard is often the most appropriate organization to lead international engagements with Caribbean nations. Panama is a case in point. Since all Panamanian armed forces were outlawed after the 1989 invasion, the U.S. military does not have a reciprocal organization with which to coordinate policy. The two most important organizations in Panama are the Panamanian National Police and the *Servicio Maritimo Nacional* (SMN)—the Panamanian Coast Guard. The police force works closely with U.S. Drug Enforcement Agency (DEA) officials to curb drug trafficking, while the SMN seeks both skilled training and technical advice from its U.S. counterpart. The utility of Coast Guard engagement is further enhanced in Panama given the transfer of the Canal on 31 December 1999 and the reluctance of the Panamanian government to allow a continued U.S. military presence in its country. There was hope in Washington that a Multilateral Counternarcotics Center could be established at Howard Air Force Base allowing the deployment of limited U.S. troops, but the Panamanian government's decision to back away from the original agreement in the summer of 1998 makes this prospect unlikely. This raises the relative importance of the Coast Guard because it is an organization that is welcomed and not shunned.

The allure of U.S. power, its successes, and its organizational professionalism can allow the United States to play a formidable role in the development of Caribbean maritime services. As Caribbean nations look more and more to the United States in general, and the Coast Guard in particular, for training and support, this soft power can translate into hard power, or more effective reciprocal organizations capable of handling their own national security interests. This cultivation of indigenous pride and energy allows the Caribbean nations to gain a heightened sense of independence and sovereignty.

The Multi-Dimensional Coast Guard

The Coast Guard can play a powerful role in ensuring the security of Caribbean nations into the next millennium, but this cannot be accomplished unilaterally. In fact, the Coast Guard is most effective within the Joint Inter-Agency Task Force (JIATF) framework, which integrates the assets and operations of several U.S. agencies, including the Department of Defense, U.S. Customs Service, DEA, and the Coast Guard. The Coast Guard is a vital cog in this framework since it is the primary maritime law enforcement agency of the United States, the lead agency for maritime drug interdiction, and shares the lead for air interdiction with U.S. Customs.[8] Many of the very assets, however, that allow the Coast Guard to play a strong role in the Caribbean—relative numbers and size of vessels—limit how wide-reaching engagement can be. Thus, the Coast Guard complements and helps support these other agencies, which are all concerned with strengthening hemispheric security in varying ways. It is this multiagency approach that facilitates Coast Guard engagement, allowing the organization to reach its interdiction potential.

This approach to Caribbean security is furthered by a strong commitment to multilateral and multinational engagement. Whenever possible, operations and training exercises incorporate all the interested parties that are willing to cooperate. For example, during a recent Tradewinds exercise at the end of April 1999, British, Dutch, and Regional Security Service (Barbados, Antigua & Barbuda, St. Lucia, St. Kitts & Nevis, Grenada, Dominica, and St. Vincent and the Grenadines) assets joined U.S. forces. This multinational operation and others like it seek to incorporate a diverse number of actors who face similar security problems. In the process, nations better their own readiness and find that cooperating with their neighbors strengthens regional solidarity and enhances communication among nations and organizations. Most important for this discussion, however, is the increasing role of multi-mission engagement.

The Coast Guard's engagement with Caribbean nations has focused primarily on counter-drug operations, despite the wide array of missions possible. This preoccupation with narcotics interdiction produced a widespread perception among many Caribbean nations that the only reason for the United States to be actively involved was to address its own security challenges, with little concern for the security priorities of Caribbean nations themselves.[9] Recently, however, Caribbean nations have begun to accept the growing pervasiveness of the drug trade, which has placed national "sovereignty under siege."[10] Intense diplomatic efforts by the State Department have capitalized on this sentiment and brought about 20 maritime counter-drug agreements with Caribbean nations. These bilateral agreements enhance the overall effectiveness of counter-drug operations, because they provide a number of functions that help nations cooperate in their interdiction efforts.

Yet as one Coast Guard officer in the international branch of Atlantic Area Operations commented, "the greatest danger for Coast Guard engagement with Caribbean nations is that counter-drug operations are overemphasized to the detriment of other more pressing missions, often more desired by the nations themselves."[11] This growing awareness as to the importance of multi-mission engagement is critical if the security concerns of the Caribbean nations themselves are to be met.

Caribbean leaders are increasingly concerned with environmental protection. The ecological disasters of the *Exxon Valdez* and other pollution incidents have raised the visibility of environmental problems from 20 years ago. Island nations need to protect their environment not only for their own citizens but also to protect their vital tourism trade. Likewise, marine inspection of vessels helps prevent potential oil spills. Thus, during a Tradewinds exercise near Puerto Plata in April 1999, the Coast Guard and the Dominican Republic navy trained heavily on oil pollution response exercises.

Similarly, the search-and-rescue mission of the Coast Guard is consistently part of training exercises. Earlier this year, exercises with the coast guard of Trinidad & Tobago rested heavily on search-and-rescue techniques and helo-hoist maneuvers with an indigenous rescue coordination center based in Port-of-Spain. Search-and-rescue operations also have been a mainstay of interaction with the Dominican Republic Navy during Operation Halcon, which has taken place eight times over the past four years, with the most recent operation occurring in January 1999. While counter-drug interdiction has been enhanced, other security interests continue to be of the utmost importance in the Caribbean. Fortunately, the Coast Guard has begun to appreciate this broadening interest and has pursued a more multi-mission approach that caters to the security needs of Caribbean nations.

Planning for the Next Millennium

The Coast Guard also has strengthened its position in the Caribbean through two complementary programs. Once Coast Guard cutters are decommissioned, many have been and will continue to be transferred to countries in the Western Hemisphere through the Excess Defense Articles (EDA) program. The

Inter-Agency Excess Defense Articles Coordination Committee may allocate more than ten decommissioned cutters a year through 2001. The class of cutters transferred—primarily 82-foot patrol boats and 157- to 180-foot buoy tenders—are better suited for the "brown-water" mission objectives of Caribbean nations. These countries find the program of paramount importance, for this is the easiest way to build the foundation for a maritime force. This program significantly increases the level of operability for smaller nations as well. Four EDA transfers, for instance, provided Trinidad & Tobago, St. Lucia, and Antigua the opportunity to participate in exercises this past April. Other recipients of EDA transfers include Panama, Costa Rica, and the Dominican Republic.

The transfer of vessels to Caribbean nations does not translate into instant success. A follow-up program is often needed to help maintain the transferred vessels. The Haitian Coast Guard is one such example. Recently, three Haitian ships were sent to the Integrated Support Command in Miami for rehabilitation. Once the vessels were brought up to speed, they were returned to Haiti where they could then be used for future operations. It is this common story that prompted the creation of a new Caribbean Support Tender (CST), which was commissioned on 27 September 1999.

The CGC *Gentian*, a 180-foot buoy tender, is the first Coast Guard cutter to be equipped with an international crew from eight different nations. The multinational crew helps to develop further credibility and bridge gaps across the region. It will soon become the cornerstone of Coast Guard engagement in the Caribbean and will professionalize the training and maintenance assistance programs. The *Gentian* will support a number of programs including engine repair, small-boat handling, and law enforcement training, as well as carrying some spare parts and basic machinery used to make such parts. While cutters do have professional and enthusiastic trainers today, they cannot build lasting relationships and training expertise, because they conduct no more than two or three missions each year. Continuity and better operational planning will also emerge as the *Gentian* crew learns about the region, develops improved programs, and learns from past visits. Thus, the crew of the *Gentian* will become expert trainers. "The CST is the most significant advancement in Coast Guard capability internationally to date," noted Captain James Underwood, chief of operations for the Atlantic Area. "We will not only help our partners but significantly improve U.S. and multinational operations as well."[12]

Toward a New Partnership

Forging a new partnership with the Western Hemisphere will be no easy task. If U.S. policy is to achieve its pursuit of greater hemispheric partnership, it should be more attuned to the concerns of Bridgetown and Port-au-Prince than Washington. The Coast Guard is one organization that has the ability to contribute to a sincere and long-lasting partnership between the United States and the Caribbean. As Caribbean nations continue to look to the successful model of the Coast Guard for training and support in their maritime development, the softer side of U.S. power will translate into more effective indigenous organizations, capable of providing for their own national security interests. In the future, Caribbean nations increasingly will share the burden of interdiction, enhance their own sense of independence and sovereignty, and in the process embrace a more permanent sense of hemispheric community.

More importantly, U.S. policy must continue to address the transnational security threats within the hemisphere that require multinational solutions. As Secretary of State Madeleine Albright asserted, "[T]he Coast Guard is the perfect weapon for the post–Cold War world." Thus, as the keys of the Canal are passed to Panama, perhaps the keys to the 21st century can be passed to the U.S. Coast Guard, since its capabilities present an ideal solution to the challenges of the Western Hemisphere.

Notes:

1. For this thesis concerning the triumph of "liberal democracy" see Francis Fukuyama, *The End of History and the Last Man* (New York: Maxwell Macmillan International, 1992).
2. See, for example, Romero's remarks at the *Miami Herald* Conference on the Americas on 18 September 1998 and his remarks to the U.S. Air Force Academy on 23 February 1999, available on the Department of State website, http://www.state.gov.

3. This study builds on the naval classifications outlined in Edmundo Gonzalez, "Redefining U.S. Hemispheric Interests: A Bold Naval Agenda for the Twenty-First Century," *Naval War College Review* (Summer 1998): pp. 37–54, esp. Table 2.
4. Joseph S. Nye, *Bound to Lead: The Changing Nature of American Power* (New York: Basic Books, 1990).
5. Author's interview with senior Coast Guard officer at the Commander, Atlantic Area, Portsmouth, Virginia, on 27 May 1999.
6. For a good overview see Admiral James M. Loy, "The Coast Guard Is Maritime Security," Naval Institute *Proceedings* (December 1998): pp. 26–29.
7. Cited in Scott C. Truver, "The World Is Our Coastline!" *Proceedings* (June 1998): pp. 45–49.
8. See Lieutenant Michele Bouziane, "The Coast Guard, National Security, and Fisheries Law Enforcement," *Naval War College Review* (Winter 1997): pp. 125–33.
9. Author's interview with senior foreign policy official at Coast Guard Headquarters, Washington, D.C., 28 May 1999.
10. See Ivelaw L. Griffith, *Drugs and Security in the Caribbean: Sovereignty Under Siege* (University Park, Penn.: Penn State Press, 1997).
11. Author's interview with Coast Guard officer at the Commander of the Atlantic Area, Portsmouth, Virginia, 18 May 1999.
12. Author's interview at the Commander, Atlantic Area, Portsmouth, Virginia, 25 May 1999.

19 "A PERFECT FIT FOR AFRICA"

CAPT Phillip J. Heyl, USCG

Captain Phillip J. Heyl was one of the USCG's leading experts in international affairs while on active duty. The USCG is indeed a perfect fit for Africa since African navies are more like the USCG than the U.S. Navy (USN). This article demonstrates Coast Guard diplomacy at its best. It is included in this anthology because if the USCG has more people and platforms, the potential for partnership opportunities with African navies and coast guards is unlimited.

"A PERFECT FIT FOR AFRICA"

By CAPT Phillip J. Heyl, USCG, U.S. Naval Institute *Proceedings* (August 2008): 38–41.

The June 2008 deployment of the U.S. Coast Guard cutter *Dallas* (WHEC-716) to West and Central Africa marked the first multi-lateral combined maritime law enforcement operation ever conducted in Africa. And it occurred in the wake of the first bilateral agreement for maritime law enforcement between the United States and an African country. The *Dallas* was deployed as the U.S. Naval Forces Europe Africa Partnership Station (APS), an initiative to enable maritime safety and security in the region. Also participating were the Cape Verde Coast Guard and the French navy.

By most accounts, the operation was an unqualified success and may provide a template for future maritime safety and security interactions for U.S. maritime forces in Africa.

The use of a U.S. Coast Guard cutter to conduct real-world law enforcement operations with the Cape Verde Coast Guard exemplifies the service's training and preparation. The commanders of Naval Forces Europe and the U.S Sixth Fleet in October 2007 deployed the Africa Partnership Station—a seagoing unit designed to change what in the past had consisted of sporadic port visits that were often unconnected with the efforts of our European partners. The start of the APS initiative corresponded with the stand-up of U.S. Africa Command (AFRICOM) as the Department of Defense's newest unified command, and is in alignment with its mission to conduct "sustained security engagement."[1]

The Coast Guard is a perfect fit for Africa because most of the continent's navies and coast guards are similar to the U.S. service in terms of missions and vessel size. The Cape Verde deployment, for instance, includes maritime law enforcement (fisheries protection and anti-smuggling—with cargo that includes drugs, humans, and weapons), search and rescue, environmental protection, and aids to navigation: all subjects that mirror the U.S. Coast Guard's missions.

The Mission

During the underway period, the *Dallas* sailed 3,000 miles with the Cape Verde law enforcement detachment (LEDET) embarked, patrolling the island nation's territorial seas and Exclusive Economic Zone (EEZ). The combined detachments boarded six vessels, both day and night, and in the last three, Cape Verde personnel led the team. The boardings, to enforce Cape Verde law, were similar to those conducted by the U.S. Coast Guard on a daily basis within our territorial seas and EEZ. Several resulted in warnings issued by Cape Verde authorities for minor fishing vessel infractions. In one case, a fishing vessel with 150 tuna on board was transiting Cape Verde's EEZ without using the required Automatic Identification System.

West Africa is fast becoming a transit area for cocaine trafficking from South America to Europe. According to the United Nations Office on Drugs and Crime, there has been a steadily increasing trend in cocaine seizures in African waters.[2] They [the UN] estimate that approximately 40 tons of cocaine was moved through West Africa in 2007. Cape Verde's strategic location 300 miles off the West Coast of Africa puts it squarely in the transit zone. This makes it an attractive staging area for drug traffickers, who could also use the island nation to launder their profits, in a phenomenon that has occurred widely in Central America and the Caribbean transit countries.

A perennial challenge for Cape Verde has been the untold number of foreign vessels used to illegally deplete its valuable offshore fish stocks. The country's coast guard is well aware of this threat to their natural resources, and all six ships boarded during this operation were fishing vessels. Combined operations such as this one allow Cape Verdeans to conduct more aggressive fisheries protection boardings well offshore.

Areas for Growth

The Coast Guard's work with port security can augment and support both AFRICOM's and the Commander, Naval Forces Europe's efforts in Africa. The African ports are considered the economic engines of the coastal African nations and of hinterland countries that rely on maritime trade. Because of the Coast Guard's port security mission and its expertise, Congress directed the service to conduct formal foreign visits in support of the international ship and port facility security code, regulated by the International Maritime Organization. Many African nations have requested a Coast Guard assessment. While port security engagement was not part of the *Dallas'* Africa Partnership Station visit, this mission should remain a focus for future Coast Guard and APS operations.

In embarking the Cape Verde law enforcement detachment it is important to note that the operational concept included a full unit instead of a ship rider, as is the norm with bilateral operations in the Caribbean, and Central and South America. A ship rider in law enforcement terms is a representative of the host country with the authority to allow Coast Guard law enforcement teams to enforce that state's laws on its behalf. The participation of an operational detachment gave Cape Verde the opportunity to acquire valuable interaction and familiarity with U.S. procedures as well as the experience of boarding large vessels outside their territorial seas. The *Dallas*' crew also delivered law enforcement equipment—protective gear including helmets, body armor, and life vests—to outfit additional Cape Verdean boarding teams.

In addition to the capacity-building dimension, major upgrades were made to the nation's operations center that allowed its leadership to communicate in real time, using translation software, simultaneously with the *Dallas* and those coordinating the operation from Naples, Italy. This allowed closer coordination of the boarding team and immediate consultation with leadership when key legal and jurisdictional issues arose.

Creating a Blueprint

Planning and preparation were essential to this operation's success. Close interagency coordination was the factor that allowed breakthroughs to occur. As one example, the U.S. embassy in the capital, Praia, played a critical role in facilitating the signing of the bilateral agreement between the United States and Cape Verde to conduct combined maritime law enforcement operations. This milestone agreement is expected to be a blueprint for future operations with other African nations, helping them to expand their maritime domain awareness to include their entire 200-nautical-mile Exclusive Economic Zone in conjunction with the United States and other international partners.

The Cape Verde operation involved several other nations, a cornerstone principle of both AFRICOM and the Navy's global maritime partnership initiative. The French provided maritime patrol aircraft support and a naval liaison officer on board the *Dallas*. The participation of French patrol aircraft combined with a U.S. Navy P-3 proved the importance of the monitor-and-detection function to increase the effectiveness of future endeavors. Officers from Equatorial Guinea also rode the *Dallas* as observers.

Rather than simply training our African partners, the United States needs to involve them in combined exercises and operations that help them build and sustain their nations' maritime forces. The desire to protect and preserve their resources and exercise sovereignty over their waters is strong. The trans-global threats of drug and human trafficking, piracy, and terrorism require international coordination, regional cooperation, and continuing action.

Future training provided by the Navy, Coast Guard, and our international partners should be enhanced by real-world operations such as those by the *Dallas* with Cape Verde. As AFRICOM's mission statement declared, we must continue to work "in concert with other U.S. government agencies and international partners . . . to conduct military-to-military programs . . . to promote a stable and secure African environment."[3]

This Africa Partnership Station deployment to Cape Verde generated significant breakthroughs that should impact the way the United States approaches maritime security in the future. The operation clearly demonstrated that international cooperation to enhance maritime security and protect natural resources works.

Notes:

1. U.S. Africa Command (AFRICOM) located in Stuttgart, Germany, under the command of Army General William E. "Kip" Ward, attained interim operating capability on 1 October 2007 and will reach unified command status on 1 October 2008.
2. UNODC World Drug Report 2007: Cocaine Trafficking in West Africa, October 2007.
3. Because U.S. Coast Guard vessels under the tactical control of the U.S. Navy are not permitted to exercise law enforcement, it was necessary to have tactical control shifted to the Coast Guard for the *Dallas* to take law enforcement action. The Commodore, Cape Verde Interdiction Operations was delegated authority by the Coast Guard to issue Statements of No Objection for appropriate law enforcement actions during this operation.

20 "COAST GUARD FOCUSES ON NY PORT SECURITY"

Martha J. LaGuardia

Ports, Waterways, and Coastal Security (PWCS) are a core mission of the USCG and consume a large portion of the operating budget. Journalist and Coast Guard Reserve Officer Martha LaGuardia-Kotite did an outstanding job of outlining the Coast Guard's role in port security operations by using the Port of New York as a case study.

"COAST GUARD FOCUSES ON NY PORT SECURITY"

By Martha J. LaGuardia, U.S. Naval Institute *Proceedings* (October 2003): 104–6.

The 11 September 2001 terrorist attacks created many new challenges for the Coast Guard in the Port of New York. As a result, New York has become the role model for other metropolitan ports in the Coast Guard's development and execution of its homeland security missions. This summer, New York Coast Guard homeland security teams will acquire new boats outfitted with advanced technology, undergo antiterrorism training, and assist in testing armed aircraft to find new ways of defending U.S. coasts and waterways.

In early September, Marine Safety and Security Team (MSST) 91106 was established in New York. Operating as a Coast Guard Atlantic Area command, the team will operate primarily in and around the ports of New York and New Jersey, but can be deployed to other areas as part of its antiterrorist force protection mission. Modeled after Coast Guard port security units, MSSTs protect military embarkations and debarkations, enforce security zones, defend critical facilities in strategic ports, interdict illegal activities, and provide force protection. Currently, Coast Guard MSSTs operate in Washington, Virginia, California, and Texas. In preparation for standing up the New York MSST, 71 highly skilled Coast Guard men and women reported to the Atlantic Area command in June. In addition, 40 reservists will be selected for duty with the team.

Defenders

To carry out its tasks, MSST 91106 has accepted two Defender-class response boats and is scheduled to receive four more. The 800 Defenders—built by SAFE Boats International—compose the largest class of boats to be acquired in the Coast Guard's history. In the next seven years, they will be delivered nationwide to Coast Guard stations, marine safety offices, MSSTs, and training commands such as Training Center, Yorktown, Virginia. The Defenders will replace the Coast Guard's aging fleet of nonstandard boats and provide additional boats to meet the service's expanding missions. These 25-foot boats mount light machine guns, use twin outboard engines to reach speeds of more than 40 knots, and have full cabins to protect their crews from the elements. They can be transported by C-130 aircraft or trailer. Equipped with advanced navigation gear, shock mitigating seats, and communications suites that enable the crews to communicate with their homeland security partners, the Defenders are in a league of their own.

One capability added to the most recent Defender-class boat design is the scalable integrated navigation system (SINS) developed by Coast Guard electronics teams. The SINS package will be the standard navigation system and equipment for the Defender class and eventually will become standard for most Coast Guard boats.

Special Training and Organizations

In early August, MSST 91106 began specialized training at the Coast Guard Training Detachment, Marine Corps Base Camp Lejeune, North Carolina. This intensive training will enhance its already specialized boat-handling skills and give the team further expertise in port security tactics. The team will learn to operate in a tactical port security environment using special weapons to conduct waterborne antiterrorism force protection.

Sea marshals operate farther off shore and seldom are observed by the millions of commuters in and around New York harbors. Because the economic impact alone would be devastating to the city if a ship rammed a bridge or released hazardous materials, their missions include combating terrorist threats before they reach shore—primarily to ensure that large vessels coming into the port cannot be used as weapons of mass destruction. There are 66 New York sea marshals and more than half of them are reservists serving on active duty. The team works closely with the New York Police Department (NYPD), Federal Bureau of Investigation, and other federal and state agencies. It trains "hybrid" sea marshals—people able to jump back and forth from one mission to another. They are versed in law enforcement and marine safety. The sea marshals' safety qualifications include expertise in container inspection and examination of foreign freighters and tankers. They are required to spend a week riding merchant vessels as part of an immersion program designed to strengthen their knowledge of vessel operations.

On an average day, the Coast Guard Activities New York Vessel Traffic Service Branch tracks more than 900 vessel movements in and around New York harbor. It is the busiest port in the nation for petroleum product movement and the third busiest for movement of containerized cargo. Vessels include oil and chemical tankers, barges, large cruise ships, and ferries of all sizes. Sea marshals will board and inspect any craft designated as a high-interest vessel. They inspect vessels and check crew lists and documentation. Stowaways are sometimes found and promptly turned over to the Immigration and Naturalization Service. In worst-case scenarios, the sea marshals are prepared to take control of a vessel without the crew's cooperation. In an emergency, they can stop a vessel several ways and prevent it from being used as a weapon.

This past summer, sea marshals and officers of the NYPD Counterterrorism Bureau conducted cross training in various tasks to gain familiarity with each other's tactics and operating environments. The NYPD High-Intensity Drug Trafficking Area Task Force provided a course that included classes on sources of funds for terrorism, fraudulent documents, crime scene preservation, cults and extremist behavior, and risk assessment. The sea marshal team also received orientation from the Coast Guard K-9 dog handlers who board containerships to detect drugs, stowaways, and dangerous cargo. The First Coast Guard District is researching the possibility of providing the New York sea marshals with their own boarding vessels. Because the 41-foot utility boats used currently are not designed to come alongside a merchant vessel, they are subject to damage in heavy seas.

The New York sea marshals have started a new program of "community policing" on state ferries. This involves meeting one-on-one with the commuters of the region to increase their awareness of the Coast Guard and its many missions. A reserve Coast Guardsman commented that he is thanked routinely while on this duty—as a Massachusetts policeman, he was never thanked by anyone.

Offshore Airborne Security

Following the 11 September terrorist attacks, the Coast Guard searched for additional ways to measure its capabilities and apply them to homeland security roles off the nation's coasts. One concept that emerged from the examination was an airborne security role for Coast Guard HH-60J Jayhawk helicopters. This summer, aircrews from the Coast Guard's First District Air Station in Cape Cod, Massachusetts, will conduct proof-of-concept tests to determine how the knowledge learned by the Helicopter Interdiction Tactical Squadron (HITRON) based in Jacksonville, Florida, can be applied to large ports.

The HITRON uses armed helicopters to interdict and apprehend drug runners in "go-fast" boats. Since the squadron began operations in 1999 following proof-of-concept testing, the drug-running situation off the Florida coast has changed perceptibly—seizures of cocaine and marijuana are valued at more than $1.7 billion. Unlike other Coast Guard aviation units, the HITRON is trained for a single mission: maritime airborne law enforcement. Squadron personnel credit much of their successful training and mission accomplishment to assistance provided by Marine Light-Attack Helicopter Squadron 269 at Marine Corps Air Station New River, North Carolina. Although Coast Guard planners recognize major hurdles in converting armed helicopters to domestic roles, they are confident the lessons learned from testing will enable them to establish the future use of airborne force in maritime homeland security.

Conclusions

The port of New York will continue to be a primary Coast Guard focal point for maritime homeland security. Representative Jim Turner (D-Texas), ranking member of the House Select Committee on Homeland Security, visited New York in May. After a helicopter overflight of the extensive operational area of responsibility, he noted: "Obviously it is a major job to protect the critical infrastructure here, and it seems that the adjustments that have been made since September 11th have put us in a better position than before. The scope of the challenges in New York exceeds anything I've seen before, and the Coast Guard is a critical part of our effort to protect the ports and waterways."

21 "READINESS IS MORE THAN NUMBERS"

ADM James M. Loy, USCG

No Coast Guard book would be complete without the wisdom of the twenty-first Commandant of the U.S. Coast Guard, Admiral James M. Loy, USCG. Readiness is essential to the Coast Guard being able to perform its myriad missions. Readiness is also one of the first things cut in austere budget climates such as the Coast Guard has had to endure for most of the past fifty years. Unfortunately, readiness issues are nothing new to the Coast Guard. Admiral Loy uses as a case study an October 1999 SAR case out of Sacramento, California, involving a C-130 aircraft.

"READINESS IS MORE THAN NUMBERS"

By ADM James M. Loy, USCG, U.S. Naval Institute *Proceedings* (February 2000): 42–45.

Dave Thomas, the fellow who founded the Wendy's hamburger chain, wrote a book about his meandering path to success. In that book, he briefly explained his approach to measuring the health of his company. As you might imagine, Mr. Thomas did not spend a lot of time poring over spreadsheets. He identified a very small set of numbers that gave him a good sense of what was going on, and he checked those numbers briefly every day. Then he spent the bulk of his energy out on the floor with his customers and employees, exercising the kind of hands-on leadership needed to keep the numbers heading in the direction he wanted. These few numbers tracked carefully—combined with a lot of personal involvement—were all he needed to have a clear grasp of where he stood.

Those of us in the readiness business quickly encounter problems when we try to follow Mr. Thomas's worthy example. If a small set of numbers exists that can convey an accurate sense of overall military readiness, it has so far eluded the most determined efforts to find it. Three important differences between hamburger stands and armed forces keep us from nailing down a convenient index of readiness.

The first difference between Dave's way and our way is that businesses measure results whereas military planners measure potential. Instead of measuring what we have done—how many hamburgers we sold and how much money we get to keep—we try to measure surge capacity: what level of effort could we amass if faced with an emergency?

A second difference is that extraordinary human effort can undermine the apparent reliability of the measures that do portray our readiness condition. The devotion to duty so prevalent among service members often puts the lie to our honest claims of reduced capability. We saw that happen some months ago, when Hurricanes Dennis and Floyd hit the eastern seaboard. The public saw the Coast Guard at the center of a massive and well-coordinated relief effort. What they didn't see was the scramble to locate parts and perform maintenance to get all of our Elizabeth City C-130s operational and to keep them flying throughout the operation. Their performance could not have been predicted from analyzing our availability statistics, and we shouldn't kid ourselves into believing that we can expect similar results as a matter of course.

A third difference is that our measures resist aggregation. No matter how big a hamburger chain grows, you can combine the financial statements of the individual units, look at the totals and the ratios between various lines, and get an idea of the overall strength. It is a lot harder to see what combinations of military units might be able to do if they are needed to work together.

The difficulty of measuring potential output quickly leads to the even more daunting challenge of explaining the basis for our readiness concerns to the American public, the administration, and to Congress. But if we look in detail at a single operational community within the Coast Guard—our fleet of C-130 aircraft—we can see how our parts shortages, personnel issues, and increased operational tempo are serious individual problems that compound the effects of the other problems.

The C-130s are a good case study for three reasons:

- They are a common currency among the armed services. Everybody flies them, so the lessons they offer may resonate more broadly than those of systems unique to the Coast Guard. C-130s are the class of Coast Guard operating assets that is most dependent on Department of Defense (DoD) systems. Many of the stresses we feel are downstream manifestations of pain that is also felt by DoD.
- C-130s are a microcosm of the readiness problems that face every operational community within the Coast Guard. The combination of aging assets and sensors, increased operational tempo, personnel shortages and inexperience, and parts shortages that besets our C-130s also hinders the effectiveness of our cutters and our other aircraft.
- C-130s epitomize previously stable trend lines that now are headed in the wrong direction. Four or five years ago, C-130s were our most reliable platform; now we struggle to meet even our normal day-to-day commitments.

Operational Tempo, Parts, and People

Several trend lines raise serious concerns. Over the past four years, HC-130 availability has dropped from almost 80% to barely 60%. Air Station Elizabeth City, North Carolina, has five C-130s, and they are expected to have one of them immediately available at all times. During the first six months of 1998, they met that standard for all but one hour. During the first six months of 1999, the hours without a ready plane jumped to 37. A standard we used to achieve easily now seems unattainable. Elizabeth City hasn't gone a single month without a coverage gap in more than a year.

Operational tempo looms as one cause. We have always worked our C-130s hard. They're getting old. They fly low-altitude patrols in a salty environment, and we program them to fly about one-third more hours than the DoD services do. Over the past few years, we haven't added new planes, our search-and-rescue obligations haven't been reduced, but we have asked our C-130s to perform a lot of deployments in support of our drug interdiction mission. As a result, C-130 days away from home station have increased more than 60% over the past four years.

We have lost a full 25% of our availability while piling on additional mission requirements. That one-two punch consumes a lot of flexibility and surge capacity.

Operational tempo feeds our parts problems. Older assets worked harder break more often. When they do, they need more parts—parts that are becoming more scarce and more expensive. We try to keep the percentage of hours for which aircraft are not mission-capable because of parts to less than 5%. Before 1995, we were consistently at or near this standard. Since then, our parts-related unavailability has risen steadily, standing now at about 16%. Over this same period, the inventory value of C-130 parts awaiting repair or replacement has doubled.

As budgets increase more slowly than costs, the problem reaches crisis proportions and desperately improvident measures suddenly seem reasonable and necessary. We look for other sources of funds—places such as the training budget—and we cannibalize parts from otherwise serviceable aircraft to keep others flying.

Experienced aviators recall times when cannibalization simply was not done. Today it is almost routine for air stations to have a designated "hangar queen," out of service for months at a time because its parts have been transplanted in other air frames. Cannibalization takes planes out of the rotation, increases the workload and maintenance on the other planes, and depletes flexibility in meeting response requirements.

Worse still, cannibalization transmutes our parts shortage into personnel problems. When we cannibalize, we double the maintenance workload. The normal way for a mechanic to replace a part is to take a box off a shelf, remove the defective part, and install the new one. One part removed, one installed. With cannibalization, two parts have to be removed and two parts have to be installed. This doubled work is performed today by less experienced maintenance crews than we had working a few years ago. The average time in grade of our chief aviation mechanics has dropped 50% over the past five years. This means that less experienced crews who should be getting more training are instead performing the extra work occasioned by cannibalization.

These personnel pressures inevitably affect retention. We train our aircraft mechanics to be professionals, and they take pride in doing their jobs right. Because they are professionals, they know when we are doubling their work, and they know that cannibalization is not the right way to do their job. Sooner or later, they have to ask whether they are willing to work twice as hard as they should to get paid less than they are worth to do a job in a way that offends their professional conscience. Overworking inexperienced crews in a strong economy is not a good prescription for improving retention.

The story here is that operational tempo, parts, and personnel problems feed off each other and compound each other.

Consequences

The real-world consequences of this situation play out in our routine operations. During October, as a result of C-130 readiness problems, we missed law enforcement missions in Florida and in Alaska. We lost track of a suspected drug smuggler because maintenance issues forced a late launch. We lost training flights to search-and-rescue and law enforcement missions. C-130s left their home bases late and returned early from law enforcement deployments because of maintenance problems. We had C-130s fly search-and-rescue missions at higher than normal search altitudes to compensate for cabin cooling limitations, thereby reducing the probability of detection. And we had C-130s reduced to visual searches because their radars did not work.

When we suffer such effects in just one month of normal operations, we know we are operating without a net when called to perform major operations.

We almost had a dramatic example when Hurricane Lenny cut a swath through the Caribbean last fall. We had a deployed C-130 in the region, and like most C-130s it had deployed with exactly one crew—we cannot afford to send spares.

Just when the C-130 was needed for disaster relief operations, one of the crew members needed a root canal and was medically grounded. As it happened, the afflicted person was a basic air crewman, and the operational commander granted a waiver to fly one person short. It worked out fine. However, if almost anybody else on that crew had needed that root canal, the flight would have been canceled. Think about it: the U.S. Coast Guard, *Semper Paratus* since 1790, was one toothache away from not being able to respond to a hurricane.

One aviator recently told me, "What we're doing now is all that we can do." The frugal taxpayer may rejoice to hear this proclamation, but the stranded boater surely does not.

The commanding officer at Air Station Barbers Point in Hawaii recalls the airlift undertaken when the supertyphoon Paka hit Guam around Christmas 1997. We mounted an all-out relief effort to bring Red Cross supplies out to the western Pacific. Looking at current availability rates for his C-130s, he doubts that he could deliver an encore performance this year.

These problems also affect other armed services. Our air station in Hawaii has a long-range-intercept mission requirement to have a C-130 available in case a civilian airplane has to ditch. The air station increasingly finds itself unable to meet this requirement and has had to pass it off to Navy P-3s for as much as two days at a time. The P-3s are not as well suited for this mission, and they already have jobs. So our readiness problem ends up becoming the Navy's readiness problem.

If that had happened last week, the results could have been deadly. A general aviation plane had to make a nighttime ditching, and a C-130 was needed to get on scene to mark the ditch course with lights and to get a fix on the downed aircraft.

Air Station Sacramento Search-and-Rescue Case

Lack of readiness may already be costing lives.

In one case in October 1999, our readiness problems may have prevented us from saving a sailor. Air Station Sacramento has four C-130s. At the time of this incident, the first C-130 was the ready aircraft on immediate standby, and a second was ready to fly as a backup to the first. The third plane was deployed for counterdrug operations out of the country, and the fourth one was the hangar queen. It had been out of service since August and was being used as a parts source for the other planes.

This situation might have been tenable except that the second C-130—the backup to the ready aircraft—was overdue for some maintenance that could be extended only for a few more days before the airplane would have to be grounded. The air station had to perform the maintenance, but scheduling it required them to choose a day on which they would have no backup to the ready C-130. Not having a backup is a bad situation for a search-and-rescue unit because mariners tend not to consult our availability schedules before getting themselves lost, and some of them remain lost until multiple sorties are flown.

But there was no choice. The air station picked a day with no law enforcement patrols planned, scheduled the maintenance, and took the plane off line to perform the work. Sure enough, there was a search-and-rescue call.

Ordered to locate the source of an EPIRB [emergency position indicating radiobeacon] alarm, the ready aircraft took off, flew 500 miles off Cape Mendocino, and found a genuine distress situation. A dismasted sailboat was battling 70-mile-per-hour winds, mountainous seas, and low visibility. The boat's lone occupant was in serious trouble. The aircrew could see him through the weather from time to time, but they could not establish communications. They dropped a radio to the sailboat, but the operator was not able to retrieve it from the heavy seas. Surface units were en route, but help was hours away.

In a case such as this—crippled vessel, extreme weather, no communications—we definitely wanted to maintain continuous air presence until a cutter could arrive on scene. And we could have if our second C-130 had been ready to fly.

But it wasn't. It was being worked on, and there was no way to button it back together in time. We looked for other assets and found an Air National Guard C-130 in Portland, Oregon, but the distances involved meant that our C-130 had to head home well before the relief plane arrived.

The Air National Guard plane reached the scene as night was falling. By that time, the EPIRB had stopped transmitting. There was no sign of the sailboat, no sign of its occupant. Nothing but wind and waves and rain.

We searched for six days. We flew 11 C-130 sorties from Sacramento. We brought in a buoy tender, a medium-endurance cutter, and a high-endurance cutter with an embarked HH-65 helicopter. The Air National Guard continued to provide C-130 support, and a USNS [United States naval ship] diverted to help. A huge effort. We spent more than we did on the more publicized JFK Jr. case. All we found was some debris.

A second C-130 might not have made any difference. It is possible that the sailor would have died even if we had kept a plane overhead. But at the very least, we would have known when and where his boat went down.

This case illustrates four unacceptable consequences of our readiness situation:

- We jeopardize our own crews by sending them into situations in which we know we cannot provide a backup if they get into trouble.
- We don't have the confidence we ought to have that we are giving stricken mariners the best possible chance to be rescued.
- Our inability to do the job right the first time requires the expenditure of far more resources than would have been needed if the right assets had been available initially.
- When we finally close the case, we find our already precarious readiness posture has been further degraded by the parts and the people we burned out in the too-much-too-late rescue effort.

A readiness climate in which we habitually make extraordinary expenditures when it is too late because we cannot bring the right resources to bear when it matters is simply intolerable to me—and ought to be intolerable to the American public.

Conclusion

When that general aviation aircraft ditched out in Hawaii, everybody involved praised the downed pilot for his poise and professionalism. After being rescued, the pilot explained why he remained calm and confident throughout his ordeal. "You know if you can hang on until the next morning that you're going to make it because the Coast Guard is going to come and get you," he said. "It's just a matter of if you can hang on."

Will Rogers once said that it's not what you don't know that gets you in trouble; it's the things you know that ain't so. This civilian pilot represents the American public in that he "knows" the Coast Guard will be there to save him if he can just hang on. Unfortunately, his knowing doesn't make it so.

The readiness problems in the C-130 world mirror similar problems of similar magnitude in our other operational communities. In fact, given that our C-130 fleet is younger and better maintained than many of our cutters, it is almost inevitable. The unfavorable trends in aircraft availability, parts inventories, and crew experience challenge our ability to provide mariners in distress with the rescue services Americans have come to expect.

These problems impose two responsibilities on us. The first is to speak frankly about the seriousness and the extent of the problems we face. We cannot permit the public to learn of this situation only when we fail dramatically to provide some service the taxpayers think they paid for. Many of our readiness issues are the sort that really can be solved by throwing money at them. Twelve or thirteen million dollars to restore our parts inventories to where they were a few years ago would be a nice place to start. We should say so.

The second responsibility is to come up with better ways to think about managing our readiness challenges. Understanding that immediate relief from budgetary constraints is unlikely, we need to attend very seriously to the problems that will persist when we shake the money tree and nothing falls into our baskets. Not having enough is not a sufficient reason for not doing our best with what we have. We will all face difficult choices about balance, setting priorities, and deciding where to allocate the next dollar. We must work together to frame our understanding of the work that lies ahead.

Editor's Note

This article is adapted from remarks delivered at the Center for Naval Analyses annual conference, "Military Readiness: Meeting the Challenge," on 1 December 1999.

22 "MULTIMISSION COSTS TOO MUCH"

CAPT Bruce B. Stubbs, USCG (Ret.)

Rounding out the part of this Wheel Book on USCG missions is a discussion about the branding of the USCG as multimission. The next two chapters are two opposing articles that do a thorough job of discussing the pros and cons of the USCG being multimission. Taking the "con" position is Captain Bruce Stubbs, who is no stranger to the readers of *Proceedings* and is well known for thinking outside the box. Stubbs writes, "New operational and policy paradigms force the Coast Guard to reexamine its multimission ethos."

"MULTIMISSION COSTS TOO MUCH"

By CAPT Bruce B. Stubbs, USCG (Ret.), U.S. Naval Institute *Proceedings* (August 2004): 30–34.

"Great battles," Winston Churchill remarked, "change the entire course of events, create new standards of values, new moods, in armies and in nations." The terrorist attacks of 11 September 2001 and the subsequent wars in Afghanistan and Iraq have had such an effect on the United States and its Coast Guard.[1] The "great battle" against al-Qaeda and affiliated terrorist groups has launched two new paradigms with the power to fundamentally alter the Coast Guard:

- An operational paradigm that demands greater concentration of resources and organizational focus on counterterrorism
- A policy paradigm that redefines the Coast Guard's national defense role as one of limited overseas deployments, if any, and extremely low-end, domestic force protection

Unlike all other federal agencies, the Coast Guard has multiple functions—transportation safety, environmental protection, search and rescue, constabulary, and defense. The new operational and policy paradigms bring into question whether the service can continue in this vein. If it seeks to preserve its multi-functional status, and does not address the full implications of these two new paradigms, the Coast Guard stands to transform much of the service into little more than a physical security force and, for all intents and purposes, becomes a uniformed, and not a military, service.

New Operational Paradigm: Active Deterrence

Vice Admiral James Hull, Commander, Atlantic Area, until his retirement on 16 July 2004, has described the Coast Guard's new operational paradigm: "We used to have one boat in the barn, so to speak, and we'd bring it out and respond when called upon. It was a firehouse response. Now we're proactive. I want the bad guys to see our presence, to see our boats, to see our planes, to know we rely on intelligence and technology and say, 'Geez, I'm going to go someplace else. This isn't worth it.'"[2]

While his "firehouse" metaphor obviously does not apply to the Coast Guard's aggressive conduct of its law-enforcement missions, the admiral has brought into sharp focus a fundamental shift in Coast Guard operations since the 11 September attacks. Counterterrorism demands that the Coast Guard expand its operational paradigm from "static response" to "active deterrence" throughout the U.S. maritime domain, while still conducting its full set of pre–9/11 missions.

Active deterrence requires the Coast Guard to project a willingness and a capability to deny terrorists their objectives by making hostile acts as difficult as possible to carry out and, if an attack occurs, to prevent attainment of the group's goals. In addition, active deterrence requires the service, using primarily the authorities of the Maritime Transportation Security Act, to establish a "national maritime security regime" by developing and enforcing physical security standards for ports, ships, and the maritime industry.[3] Coast Guard operational forces must be equipped and trained for defensive activities that aim at protecting people, critical infrastructure, and key assets from terrorist attacks and for offensive activities that aim at interdicting, disrupting, and destroying terrorists that are planning to (e.g., gathering intelligence) or are on their way to attack a target. Coast Guard prevention forces, responsible for establishing the national maritime security regime, must become subject matter experts in physical security, port operations, and supply chain logistics from point of origin to destination.

All forces must be fully deployable, either in totality or in detachments, for assignments in other regions as the threat or operational conditions change. In addition, for Coast Guard forces to act as deterrents, they must have credibility that they have the skills and weapons to get the job done. Obsolescent forces or forces with a capability-to-threat mismatch have low credibility and are easily countered. Finally, these forces must be prepared for all eventualities. They must be ready for the unexpected, since they no longer can trust that "what they see is what they get." If events go sour on a boarding at sea, Coast Guard forces cannot as easily extract themselves as their land-based brethren can from a vehicle they have stopped or a building they have entered. When it comes to unexpectedly confronting a terrorist threat on a ship in the course of a "normal" boarding, Coast Guardsmen at sea are in a "Velcro boarding"—they are stuck. They need to be well trained and well equipped for counterterrorism operations.

Active deterrence shifts mission execution from relatively straightforward single-unit sorties for discrete, short-duration, maritime incidents to enduring, complex, multiagency, multiunit campaigns with detailed tasking orders against numerous, adaptive, and asymmetric threats. Operational commanders, especially those at the tactical (port and regional) level, must be supported, not only by a current operations staff, but also by separate, dedicated staffs for planning and intelligence. In lieu of focusing on reactionary operational decision-making as experienced in the firehouse model, field commanders must concentrate on developing extensive knowledge of terrorists' capabilities, methods, objectives, ideologies, and organizational structures to assess their strengths, vulnerabilities, and centers of gravity. On the basis of this understanding, they can plan and implement reliable protective measures and effective defensive and offensive operations, and identify requirements to operate against agile adversaries versus rescuing distressed boaters.

Table 1. ATTRIBUTES OF THE NEW OPERATIONAL PARADIGM

ATTRIBUTE	OLD PARADIGM "STATIC RESPONSE"	NEW PARADIGM "ACTIVE DETERRENCE"
Mission Emphasis	Humanitarian Search and Rescue	Multimission Search and Rescue Maritime Homeland Security
Mission Complexity	Low	Very High
Command & Control	Hierarchical U.S. Coast Guard	Shared Joint, Multiagency, State & Local Authorities
Information Security and Communications	Largely Internal Unclassified	Joint, Multiagency Classified
Operational Staff Focus	CG-3 (Current Ops)	CG-2 (Intel), CG-3 (Current Ops), CG-5 (Plans)
Mission Execution	Single Unit, Discrete Event, Short Duration	Detailed Tasking Orders Campaign Planning Multimission, Adaptive Force Packages Joint, Multiagency & Multiple Units
Geographic Focus	Regional/Local	National/International, Regional/Local
Force Location	Generally Fixed Associated with Fixed Site	Mobile Forward-Deployed National and International Operations
Technology	Sextant Angles COMDAC*	Digital, Integrated, Secure Networks, Info Technology, Global Positioning
"Last Full Measure"	No	Yes

*Command Display and Control Integrated Navigation System

In the most far-reaching change, interdiction of weapons of mass destruction (WMD) or terrorists en route to attack demands Coast Guard personnel be prepared to give their lives in defense of their country. It is a hard truth, but in the war on terrorism, they are expected to give their "last full measure." Just as "every Marine is a rifleman," Coast Guardsmen at all tactical units must now be trained and equipped to a baseline law-enforcement and physical-security standard—weapons and boarding team qualified at a minimum. No matter their specialty, Coast Guard personnel must be well grounded in basic maritime security tasks to defend themselves and their units. In active deterrence, few operational missions will not require Coast Guardsmen to be armed.[4]

The implications of this new operational paradigm are enormous. It will change the way the Coast Guard organizes, trains, and equips its forces, and how it plans and executes its missions. To its credit, the Coast Guard has recognized these realities and made many key adjustments:

- It has declared counterterrorism shares the same high priority as its traditional search-and-rescue mission.
- It has established a new tactical command-and-control organization to replace its fragmented arrangement of independent units with maritime "sector commands" that merge these units into one organization responsible for all missions.
- To improve training, it recently established a Maritime Law Enforcement Academy in South Carolina by relocating and fusing the Maritime Law Enforcement School in Yorktown, Virginia, and the Boarding Team Member School in Petaluma, California.
- It has established a law enforcement qualification program to increase its ability to train, grow, and retain law enforcement professionals among its enlisted rates—but did not go so far as to authorize a new and separate law enforcement rating.
- It is well on its way to standing up 13 specialized domestic physical security units, Marine Safety and Security Teams, at critical seaports.

- It commissioned Maritime Intelligence Fusion Centers at the Atlantic and Pacific Area commands, assigned Field Intelligence Support teams to vital seaports, and increased staffing at its Intelligence Coordination Center.

It is evident from the types of new units established and the nature of the terrorist threat that Coast Guard personnel involved in law enforcement, planning, security, and intelligence require greater levels of specialized skills than was the case before 11 September. They need extensive training in a host of counterterrorism and weapons subjects; frequent requalification; and something as prosaic as security clearances and physical fitness. Personnel operating aircraft and boats that deliver lethal and nonlethal fires require even more specialized training and frequent practice because of the significant consequences of errors and the danger inherent in their duties. The hundreds of persons assigned to the expanded intelligence program are an even more special case. The enlisted personnel are sourced from ratings such as yeoman, storekeeper, subsistence specialist, and marine science technician to become trained intelligence or counterterrorism analysts, with high-level security clearances, including special access. Once in the intelligence program, they can further specialize in disciplines such as imagery, electronic, or human intelligence. The upshot of all this is that a significant portion of the Coast Guard's total workforce is becoming highly specialized for maritime security duties.

New National Defense Paradigm: Guard the U.S. Coast

Through a series of actions, the Defense Department is redefining the Coast Guard's national defense function as guarding the homeland and low-end force protection responsibilities. Some key DoD leaders publicly questioned the appropriateness of the Coast Guard's deployment of 11 cutters and 4 port security units (PSUs) to the Persian Gulf for Operation Iraqi Freedom in view of the magnitude of the Coast Guard's homeland security responsibilities and the anticipated increase in the homeland threat level.[5] They pointed to the apparent paradox of Navy frigates conducting counterdrug operations and Navy patrol craft conducting domestic homeland security missions while the Coast Guard dispatched cutters to Iraq. Some Defense officials harbored additional concerns that—short of a declared war—DoD could not rely on the Coast Guard to fulfill its obligations spelled out in the combatant commanders' contingency plans because its domestic homeland security duties have precedence.

In addition, the Navy is replicating Coast Guard national defense capabilities called out in the 1995 Memorandum of Agreement between the Defense and Transportation Departments. This memorandum defines five categories of "specialized" capabilities the Coast Guard provides: (1) maritime interception operations (MIO); (2) port operations, security, and defense; (3) military environmental response; (4) peacetime military engagement (PME); and (5) coastal sea control.[6]

For each category, the Navy has either replicated the capability or can hire it elsewhere. The Navy began its own MIO by establishing boarding schools whose curricula have many similarities to those at the Coast Guard's law enforcement schools.[7] Today, the Navy's MIO capabilities are so good that a U.S.-Liberian accord signed in February 2004 authorizes the Navy to board Liberian registered commercial ships in international waters to search for WMD.[8] The Navy's mobile security squadrons (MSSs), naval coastal warfare groups, independent boat units, mobile inshore undersea warfare units, and harbor defense commands provide equivalent capabilities to the Coast Guard's for the port operations, security, and defense category and for the coastal sea control category. The MSSs, with 175 active-duty personnel operating six 25-foot patrol craft, are the Navy's version of the Coast Guard's PSUs. If DoD operational commanders need environmental response capability, they can get it from the Environmental Protection Agency or buy it from a contractor. In a similar fashion, commercial firms such as DynCorp, MPRI, or Kellogg, Brown and Root can provide PME capabilities in Coast Guard missions.

Transformation

The Coast Guard's essence is the interchangeability of its people and platforms for multiple duties. Although most federal agencies are organized around a single core function, the Coast Guard has multiple core missions. In keeping with its corporate ideology, Coast Guard personnel are assigned to a disparate range of duties, as exemplified by the recent comment of a chief petty officer: "Just a year ago, I was a boarding officer and managing an engineering team on a Coast Guard cutter. These days, I'm helping mariners navigate the challenges and consequences of drug use, and trying to prevent future marine accidents by determining what caused them."[9] This typical Coast Guardsman cites at least four different primary duty functions he has performed: (1) maritime law enforcement boarding officer; (2) senior marine engineering technician; (3) criminal investigator for drug misuse; and (4) maritime transportation safety analyst.

Being multimission has caused the Coast Guard to generalize the professional development and training of its people. For example, it is not uncommon for an officer to spend 25 years as a support specialist, be selected for admiral, and become an operational field commander, responsible for missions he has never conducted. In lieu of formal, resident training, the Coast Guard counts on on-the-job training and professional qualifications standards for the majority of its law enforcement personnel, and unlike DoD, it does not require joint professional military education (JME) for its officers, but it expects to be integrated into military operations and commands in the same manner as the other services. The multimission doctrine obliges the Coast Guard to place a greater value on being a generalist than a specialist and to treat those who do support missions as interchangeable with those who do operational missions. Unfortunately, one very harmful result of this doctrine is that other federal agencies, especially the law enforcement agencies and the other military services, have mixed views of the Coast Guard's competencies.[10]

The Coast Guard acknowledges that the costs of maintaining a multimission force are too high. Prior to 11 September, plans were afoot to remove all weapons but side arms from operational shore units with small boats. In a cost-cutting move, the Coast Guard already had removed chemical, biological, and radiological capabilities from its cutters. And when 200 Haitians sailed brazenly into Miami harbor in fall 2002, the first Coast Guard unit to spot them and attempt an interdiction was a single-mission, aids-to-navigation vessel with no law-enforcement capabilities; it consequently failed in the attempt.

As the Coast Guard embraces this new operational paradigm, the increased demand for a specialized workforce devoted to maritime security and the associated costs of maintaining workforce competency preclude multimission career paths for most Coast Guardsmen. It is imprudent operationally and economically to assign highly skilled and trained law enforcement and intelligence personnel with special security clearances to unrelated duty assignments such as boating safety, icebreaking, repairing aids to navigation, oil spill containment, or personnel management.

DoD is sending the Coast Guard a message to stay home and guard the coasts. Underscoring that message is a Navy policy to replicate Coast Guard "non-redundant capabilities" and its less than full commitment to fund the combat systems for all new Coast Guard Deepwater cutters. The Coast Guard's national defense role is being redefined as one of little relevancy and value to the Defense Department. Aside from the 1995 Memorandum of Agreement, DoD leaders have thought so little of the Coast Guard's national defense contribution that they have never acknowledged the Coast Guard's national defense role in any formal planning or reporting document, such as the Secretary of Defense's Annual Report to the President and the Congress.[11]

An Unaffordable Ethos

New operational and policy paradigms force the Coast Guard to reexamine its multimission ethos. It no longer can afford the training costs; the nation cannot risk "generalists" going in harm's way against the likes of al-Qaeda; and in attempting to be all things to all people, the Coast Guard sets capabilities and personnel expertise for many of its missions to a baseline level. DoD has pounced on this shortcoming. It perceives a major gap in our national capabilities for domestic maritime interdiction. The Commander, U.S. Northern Command, questions whether the Coast Guard can deal with terrorists smuggling a WMD into the country on a vessel.[12] The Chief of Naval Operations wants "a maritime NORAD" [North American Aerospace Defense Command] and has stood up a Navy working group to do just that.[13]

The attacks of 11 September 2001 were a defining moment for the Coast Guard. Its expanded role in homeland security and its relocation to the Department of Homeland Security will not be reversed. By maintaining its emphasis on its multimission doctrine, and underestimating the full implications of these two new paradigms, the Coast Guard transforms a large portion of the service into a domestic, paramilitary guard force, forfeits its status as a valued member of the nation's defense team, and loses the lead for maritime security—at home as well as overseas.

Notes

1. Victor Davis Hanson, *Ripples of Battle* (New York: Doubleday, 2003).
2. David Lamb, "Coast Guard's Status Is on a Rising Tide," *Los Angeles Times*, 8 February 2004.
3. Joint Statement of Adm. Thomas H. Collins, Commandant, U.S. Coast Guard; Robert C. Bonner, Commissioner, Customs and Border Protection; and Rear Adm. David M. Stone, USN (Ret.), Acting Administrator, Transportation Security Administration, Department of Homeland Security, on Maritime Security Status before the Committee on Commerce, Science, and Transportation, U.S. Senate, 24 March 2004.
4. This does not mean the entire Coast Guard is trained and equipped for the full range of counterterrorism operations. Instead, specialized quick-reaction units provide enhanced capabilities (e.g., lethality, vertical insertion, opposed boardings).
5. John Mintz and Vernon Loeb, "Coast Guard Fights to Retain War Role," *Washington Post*, 31 August 2003, p. A07. As the *Washington Post* reported, some Defense and Navy officials suggested that the Coast Guard restrict itself to "guarding the coast"; that overseas deployments of Coast Guard units be "written out" of current DoD operational plans; and that the Navy begin developing organic equivalents for many of the capabilities now provided by the Coast Guard, such as maritime interception and port security in forward areas.
6. Revised DoD and DoT "Memorandum of Agreement on the Use of U.S. Coast Guard Capabilities and Resources in Support of the National Military Strategy," 3 October 1995.
7. At these schools, "students learn to embark and debark foreign vessels to review documents, and inspect the vessel, its cargo and personnel. Students

also learn to identify and control threats and hazards, collect evidence and intelligence information, and manage medical emergencies." JO2 Sean A. Hughes, USN, "Navy, Coast Guard Team Up for Boarding, Search and Seizure Training." Commander in Chief, U.S. Pacific Fleet website news item, undated [http://www.cpf.navy.mil/news.aspx/].

8. Edward Harris, "U.S. Navy Gets OK to Search All Liberian-Flagged Ships for WMD," Associated Press, 13 February 2004.
9. Lt. Cdr. Todd Offutt, USCG, "Coast Guard 'Columbo,'" *Hawai'i Navy News*, 12 March 2004.
10. Because of the Coast Guard's training methods and because the Coast Guard does not conduct investigations, federal agencies are reluctant to authorize armed Coast Guard personnel to conduct missions on land without elaborate and special provisions—something the Coast Guard urgently requires to improve its security posture in the ports and waterways.
11. The Navy also has not supported the Senate and House Armed Services Committees receiving any testimony or even informal briefings on the Coast Guard's national defense capabilities, the National Fleet policy, or the Deepwater Project.
12. Chris Strohm, "Military Explores Greater Role in Maritime Security," *GovExec .com*, 3 March 2004.
13. Marnes W. Crawley, "Top Admiral Urges 'Maritime NORAD' for Security on Seas," *San Diego Union Tribune*, 5 February 2004.

23 "NOW, MORE THAN EVER: A MULTIMISSION COAST GUARD"

VADM Terry Cross, USCG

Coast Guard Vice Commandant Vice Admiral Terry Cross' June 2005 *Proceedings* article was in response to Captain Bruce Stubbs' article that appears in the previous chapter of this Wheel Book. Vice Admiral Cross took the pro-multimission position with the view, "Multimission capabilities, interagency partnerships, and unique authorities lead to operational flexibility and mission success." A healthy debate on the quantity of the USCG's 11 statutory missions occurred on the pages of *Proceedings*—a debate worth having given the limited resources made available to the USCG.

"NOW, MORE THAN EVER: A MULTIMISSION COAST GUARD"

By VADM Terry Cross, USCG, U.S. Naval Institute *Proceedings* (June 2005): 38–40.

The Report of the Interagency Task Force on U.S. Coast Guard Roles and Missions dated December 1999 stated that, "The U.S. will continue to need a flexible, adaptable, multimission, military Coast Guard to meet national maritime interests and requirements well into the next century."[1] The assertion was valid then, and it is no less valid now in the post–9/11 security environment. Over the past three years, the nation's multimission Coast Guard demonstrated remarkable responsiveness, initiative, and flexibility, while systematically improving our nation's maritime homeland security. It engaged the enemy abroad, provided for the common defense at home, and otherwise served the broad spectrum of the nation's maritime interests with distinction.

An essay by Captain Bruce Stubbs, U.S. Coast Guard (Ret.), titled "Multimission Costs Too Much," in the August 2004 *Proceedings*, proposes that the nation cannot afford such a service. The author states that two paradigm shifts argue for a service focused more on counterterrorism: "An operational paradigm that demands greater concentration of resources and organizational focus on counterterrorism, [and] a policy paradigm that redefines the Coast Guard's national defense role as one of limited overseas deployments, if any, and extremely low-end, domestic force protection."[2] He believes that our multifaceted capabilities erode a needed focus on counterterrorism.

I respectfully disagree. The nation should not want—and could not afford—a single-mission Coast Guard. Moreover, it is precisely the force's authorities, capabilities, and partnerships that led Secretary Tom Ridge to designate it as the lead federal agency for Maritime Homeland Security in 2002.

Despite the operational demands that came with the increased attention to port, waterway, and coastal security, our organization continued to protect the public, the environment, and U.S. economic interests in many diverse ways. (See box.)

These are daily resource-intensive actions, not exercises. They reflect the realities of the never-ending stream of typical days in the life of our maritime nation and the Coast Guard. Moreover, while accomplishing the missions reflected in the statistics, the Coast Guard remains always ready to respond to a national crisis, be it a natural disaster, mass migration of illegal migrants, or a national security event, every day, in all weather conditions, at a moment's notice. What governmental agency, private enterprise, or public endeavor could deliver this type of single-provider response and return on investment to the American taxpayer?

An Illusory Argument

The contention that the Coast Guard lacks the funds to be a multimission service but would somehow have sufficient funds if it focused on counterterrorism operations is illusory. While I agree that sustaining present and future readiness is a daunting funding challenge given aging cutter and aircraft fleets, the administration and Congress have significantly increased funding. The key element here is that its missions are either mandated or authorized by statute and funded by Congress. Any missions transferred from it would have to be accomplished by other agencies. With mission transfers, the supporting people, equipment, and funds would inevitably follow. The result would be a much smaller and poorer Coast Guard. Additionally, inefficiencies associated with having several agencies working to accomplish maritime missions, now done by the service, would increase the overall cost. Higher costs and lower operational returns argue against dismantling the current organization.

The Ideal Agency

Post 9/11, it was generally recognized throughout government that the Coast Guard's multimission character made it the ideal agency to lead the nation's maritime homeland security effort. Its multimission character is a benefit—not a distraction—in the war on terror. The Maritime Homeland Security Strategy aligns with the president's and Department of Homeland Security's goals. Our strategy leverages the Coast Guard's unique authorities, capacity, partnerships, and capabilities. It has the government's broadest maritime authorities through its roles as a military service, a federal law enforcement agency, and a federal regulatory agency. Its authorities permit it to control the entry of vessels into and out of U.S. ports and their movement on our waters, and to board and inspect vessels in U.S. waters without probable cause. New authorities in the Maritime Transportation Security Act of 2002 designate Coast Guard Captains of the Port as heads of Port Security Committees and direct the service to set and enforce standards for ship and port facility security plans. Losing these or related authorities by eliminating non-homeland security missions would decrease the service's effectiveness in the war on terror.

Clearly, the Coast Guard needed more capacity to adequately address substantially expanded post–9/11 Maritime Homeland Security responsibilities, and it has grown substantially. Thus far, its workforce has increased about 13% and it has added hundreds of small boats, including 19 patrol craft. Nevertheless, it was the Coast Guard's multimission character that allowed it to respond in great force immediately following the terrorist attacks, when hundreds of units shifted missions and became homeland security units. The inclusion of buoy tenders and hundreds of other Coast Guard boats in the fleet dramatically increases the presence and deterrent capability in our ports, waterways, and offshore.

Decades of Cooperation and Coordination

Partnerships are also important. Most senior Pentagon officers now embrace the idea that in future wars, just being joint will not suffice. Effectiveness in the global war on terror will also require increased interagency cooperation and coordination. The Coast Guard, by necessity and practice, has been both joint and interagency for decades. There are virtually no users of the nation's exclusive economic zone, waterways, or ports that do not routinely engage and communicate with it. It enjoys a strong working relationship with the Navy and works closely with the other services as required, including the Army Corps of Engineers to manage the nation's inland waterways. The Coast Guard frequently works with other federal agencies including Border and Transportation Security, Federal Emergency Management Agency, Secret Service, Federal Bureau of Investigation, and the National Oceanographic and Atmospheric Administration. It teams with state and local first responders for search and rescue, pollution response, and law enforcement missions. Its law enforcement, regulatory, and marine safety functions require ongoing relationships with the international and domestic marine industry, port operators, pilots, fishing industry, and recreational boaters; all vital partners in the war on terror. Many of the service's partners work, and some even live, on the water. They are terrific force multipliers. Finally, we are members of the intelligence community and long-time partners with the Office of Naval Intelligence. The Coast Guard already works the way others wish they could work and enjoys relationships others wish they could experience because we are multimission.

In the past year, the Coast Guard teamed with federal, state, and local agencies to provide antiterrorism protection during both national political conventions and the G-8 Summit, management responses in the wake of four major hurricanes, record-breaking cocaine seizures, and a successful no-notice operation to stem a potential mass migration from Haiti.

Consider how its multimission character and interagency relationships supported border security operations during the Haitian crisis. From fishery patrols in the North Atlantic to counter-narcotics patrols in the deep Caribbean, cutters raced to prevent a mass migration from Haiti. There were no stops for additional people, training, supplies, or direction. All cutters and crews responded fully mission capable. In addition, the Department of Homeland Security stood up the Homeland Security Task Force–Southeast, a fully integrated interagency task force, to direct U.S. efforts to manage the crisis, with the Coast Guard Seventh District Commander as the director. Further, Southern Command designated the service as the Maritime Component Commander. The results of this joint effort, predicated on interagency cooperation and advance planning, were exceptional. No Haitian migrants reached U.S. shores or lost their lives at sea.

The World's Model

The Coast Guard's unique blend of military, law enforcement, and regulatory responsibilities has made its multimission organization attractive to nations around the world. Because many foreign navies and coast guards mirror the U.S. Coast Guard's multifaceted portfolio, it receives frequent requests to help other nations exercise and train their maritime forces. Enhancing the professionalism of maritime services around the world contributes to global security and builds trust and confidence among our international partners.

Captain Stubbs' article was correct to point out that the Coast Guard needs more capability to effectively fight the terror threat. He recognized its many advances since 9/11 in organization (Sectors), intelligence (Field Intelligence Support Teams), response units (Marine Safety and Security Teams), and capabilities (Aerial Use of Force).

A TYPICAL COAST GUARD DAY

- Provided a catalog of services throughout 3.4 million square miles of the U.S. Exclusive Economic Zone and beyond
- Supported Operation Iraqi Freedom with deployed forces
- Boarded four high-interest vessels before they entered U.S. ports
- Enforced 129 security zones protecting critical infrastructure
- Conducted 23 waterfront facility safety or security inspections
- Responded to 90 search and rescue calls, saving 15 lives and assisting 117 other people in distress, and protected property valued at over $2,827,397
- Conducted 98 port security patrols and 52 security boardings
- Flew 19 air patrols in support of homeland security
- Boarded 192 vessels for law enforcement
- Seized 662 pounds of cocaine worth $21,095,890 and 71 pounds of marijuana
- Interdicted and rescued 30 illegal immigrants
- Facilitated the transit of 2,557 commercial ships entering and leaving port
- Cleared the way for 12 vessels carrying bulk materials and fuel products in ice conditions
- Provided ice safety information to facilitate 1,128,235 tons of cargo shipped daily during the North Atlantic ice season
- Conducted 317 vessel safety checks and taught 63 safe boating courses
- Opened 27 cases for marine violation of federal statutes
- Processed 280 seaman licenses and documents
- Boarded 122 large vessels for port safety/security checks
- Conducted 19 commercial vessel safety exams and issued seven fishing vessel decals
- Responded to 11 environmental pollution incidents totaling 2,181 gallons
- Investigated 20 vessel casualties involving collisions, groundings or fires

To complement these successes, the Coast Guard needs modern cutter and aircraft fleets that reflect post-9/11 realities. The growing requirement for its services is exceeding the capacity and capabilities of its aging and technologically obsolete assets. For example, of the world's 41 naval fleets, only those of Mexico and the Philippines are older than the Coast Guard's. Critical, ongoing acquisitions are essential to our ability to build and maintain operational excellence across the full range of missions.

The Integrated Deepwater System is needed to replace surface and air assets and to put in place a C^4ISR infrastructure that increases maritime domain awareness. The Deepwater project complements Rescue 21 and Command 2010, the service's efforts to update critical inshore command and control capability. Deepwater is essential to its ability to provide a defense in depth capability and to meet the challenges of our Maritime Homeland Security Strategy. Maritime domain awareness and Deepwater will ensure that the Coast Guard and our nation will be able to meet threats, not at the sea buoy when it is too late, but far at sea where it can provide the National Command Authority time to develop options and engage the enemy on our terms.

The author's policy paradigm shift relates to the Coast Guard's expeditionary role. The service has long been a niche player in overseas military engagements. That is as it should be. Further, DoD's recent focus on realigning itself in the post–9/11 environment is more than appropriate, it is necessary. The DoD/CG team is stronger than ever, in particular the USN/CG team. We will support each other's missions in a manner consistent with our authorities, competencies, and capabilities. Our joint effort to define and execute a maritime security strategy rightly focuses on each service's ability to expand our awareness and identify potential responses to terrorist acts. In addition, joint Coast Guard, Navy, federal law enforcement, and national intelligence agency efforts in the war on drugs is paying dividends in the war on terror. Last year, the Coast Guard seized more than $7.7 billion dollars worth of cocaine—that is money not financing terrorists and criminal organizations worldwide. Clearly, multi-mission capability makes our nation safer.

A Multimission Coast Guard Is a Necessity

Captain Stubbs' concern that the service's multimission character "forfeits its status as a valued member of the nation's defense team, and loses the lead for maritime security—at home as well as overseas" is misplaced. On the contrary, a strong, viable, multimission Coast Guard, with an infusion of new and more capable ships, aircraft, and C^4ISR, will provide the necessary force structure needed to maintain our quality of life through the security of our maritime borders, the free flow of maritime trade, and continued support to the public and private maritime community. The nation's maritime strategy balances the service's responsibility for upholding America's maritime security against the terrorist threat with the imperatives of preserving our fundamental liberties and economic well-being. Multimission capabilities, interagency partnerships, and unique authorities lead to operational flexibility and mission success. Now more than ever, the nation needs its multimission Coast Guard.

Notes

1. "A Coast Guard for the Twenty-first Century," Executive Summary to Report of the Interagency Task Force on U.S. Coast Guard Roles and Missions (December 1999): vii.
2. Bruce Stubbs, "Multimission Costs Too Much," *Proceedings* (August 2004): 30–34.

INDEX

ABOUT THE EDITOR

Jim Dolbow is editor of *The Coast Guardsman's Manual, 11th Edition*, published by the Naval Institute Press, and a former member of the U.S. Naval Institute Editorial Board from 2005 to 2010. From 2002 to 2010, he served as a drilling reservist in the U.S. Coast Guard Reserve. Dolbow is presently a senior acquisitions editor for professional development books at the U.S. Naval Institute and a Fleet Professor of Theater Decision Making for the U.S. Naval War College's Fleet Seminar Program in Washington, D.C.

A lifelong student of national security affairs, Dolbow has studied and trained at the Institute of World Politics, the U.S. Naval War College, Joint Special Operations University, and the U.S. Air Force Special Operations School. A frequent writer, he has been published in *Proceedings*, *National Defense*, the *Washington Post*, *Washington Times*, *Sea Power*, *Navy Times*, and the *Armed Forces Journal International*, among others. In 2013 he was awarded first prize with CAPT Jim Howe, USCG (Ret.), as *Proceedings* Authors of the Year. He is the proud owner of Conan, a rescued Black and Tan Coonhound.

The Naval Institute Press is the book-publishing arm of the U.S. Naval Institute, a private, nonprofit, membership society for sea service professionals and others who share an interest in naval and maritime affairs. Established in 1873 at the U.S. Naval Academy in Annapolis, Maryland, where its offices remain today, the Naval Institute has members worldwide.

Members of the Naval Institute support the education programs of the society and receive the influential monthly magazine *Proceedings* or the colorful bimonthly magazine *Naval History* and discounts on fine nautical prints and on ship and aircraft photos. They also have access to the transcripts of the Institute's Oral History Program and get discounted admission to any of the Institute-sponsored seminars offered around the country.

The Naval Institute's book-publishing program, begun in 1898 with basic guides to naval practices, has broadened its scope to include books of more general interest. Now the Naval Institute Press publishes about seventy titles each year, ranging from how-to books on boating and navigation to battle histories, biographies, ship and aircraft guides, and novels. Institute members receive significant discounts on the Press's more than eight hundred books in print.

Full-time students are eligible for special half-price membership rates. Life memberships are also available.

For a free catalog describing Naval Institute Press books currently available, and for further information about joining the U.S. Naval Institute, please write to:

Member Services
U.S. NAVAL INSTITUTE
291 Wood Road
Annapolis, MD 21402-5034
Telephone: (800) 233-8764
Fax: (410) 571-1703
Web address: www.usni.org